OPPOSING
VIEWPOINTS®
SERIES

D0380670

| Ethics

Other Books of Related Interest:

Opposing Viewpoints Series
Atheism

Genetic Engineering

Religion in America

War Crimes

Current Controversies Series
Human Genetics

Human Trafficking

Medical Ethics

At Issue Series
Embryonic and Adult Stem Cells

The Ethics of Cloning

Is Selling Body Parts Ethical?

The Right to Die

"Congress shall make
no law . . . abridging
the freedom of speech,
or of the press."

First Amendment to the U.S. Constitution

The basic foundation of our democracy is the First Amendment guarantee of freedom of expression. The Opposing Viewpoints Series is dedicated to the concept of this basic freedom and the idea that it is more important to practice it than to enshrine it.

OPPOSING VIEWPOINTS® SERIES

Ethics

Roman Espejo, Book Editor

GREENHAVEN PRESS
A part of Gale, Cengage Learning

GALE
CENGAGE Learning™

Detroit • New York • San Francisco • New Haven, Conn • Waterville, Maine • London

Christine Nasso, *Publisher*
Elizabeth Des Chenes, *Managing Editor*

© 2010 Greenhaven Press, a part of Gale, Cengage Learning

Gale and Greenhaven Press are registered trademarks used herein under license.

For more information, contact:
Greenhaven Press
27500 Drake Rd.
Farmington Hills, MI 48331-3535
Or you can visit our Internet site at gale.cengage.com

For product information and technology assistance, contact us at

Gale Customer Support, 1-800-877-4253
For permission to use material from this text or product, submit all requests online at
www.cengage.com/permissions

Further permissions questions can be emailed to permissionrequest@cengage.com

Articles in Greenhaven Press anthologies are often edited for length to meet page requirements. In addition, original titles of these works are changed to clearly present the main thesis and to explicitly indicate the author's opinion. Every effort is made to ensure that Greenhaven Press accurately reflects the original intent of the authors. Every effort has been made to trace the owners of copyrighted material.

Cover image copyright Rybakov Vadim Grigor'evich, 2010. Used under license from Shutterstock.com.

LIBRARY OF CONGRESS CATALOGING-IN-PUBLICATION DATA

Ethics / Roman Espejo, book editor.
    p. cm. -- (Opposing viewpoints)
    Includes bibliographical references and index.
    ISBN 978-0-7377-4767-6 (hardcover) -- ISBN 978-0-7377-4768-3 (pbk.)
  1. Ethics--Textbooks. I. Espejo, Roman, 1977-
  BJ1025.E825 2010
  170--dc22
                                      2009053382

Printed in the United States of America
1 2 3 4 5 6 7 14 13 12 11 10

Contents

Chapter 3: Are Modern Biomedical Practices Ethical?

Chapter 4: Are Ethics in Business Practices Beneficial?

Why Consider Opposing Viewpoints?

> *"The only way in which a human being can make some approach to knowing the whole of a subject is by hearing what can be said about it by persons of every variety of opinion and studying all modes in which it can be looked at by every character of mind. No wise man ever acquired his wisdom in any mode but this."*
>
> *John Stuart Mill*

In our media-intensive culture it is not difficult to find differing opinions. Thousands of newspapers and magazines and dozens of radio and television talk shows resound with differing points of view. The difficulty lies in deciding which opinion to agree with and which "experts" seem the most credible. The more inundated we become with differing opinions and claims, the more essential it is to hone critical reading and thinking skills to evaluate these ideas. Opposing Viewpoints books address this problem directly by presenting stimulating debates that can be used to enhance and teach these skills. The varied opinions contained in each book examine many different aspects of a single issue. While examining these conveniently edited opposing views, readers can develop critical thinking skills such as the ability to compare and contrast authors' credibility, facts, argumentation styles, use of persuasive techniques, and other stylistic tools. In short, the Opposing Viewpoints Series is an ideal way to attain the higher-level thinking and reading skills so essential in a culture of diverse and contradictory opinions.

In addition to providing a tool for critical thinking, Opposing Viewpoints books challenge readers to question their own strongly held opinions and assumptions. Most people form their opinions on the basis of upbringing, peer pressure, and personal, cultural, or professional bias. By reading carefully balanced opposing views, readers must directly confront new ideas as well as the opinions of those with whom they disagree. This is not to argue simplistically that everyone who reads opposing views will—or should—change his or her opinion. Instead, the series enhances readers' understanding of their own views by encouraging confrontation with opposing ideas. Careful examination of others' views can lead to the readers' understanding of the logical inconsistencies in their own opinions, perspective on why they hold an opinion, and the consideration of the possibility that their opinion requires further evaluation.

Evaluating Other Opinions

To ensure that this type of examination occurs, Opposing Viewpoints books present all types of opinions. Prominent spokespeople on different sides of each issue as well as well-known professionals from many disciplines challenge the reader. An additional goal of the series is to provide a forum for other, less known, or even unpopular viewpoints. The opinion of an ordinary person who has had to make the decision to cut off life support from a terminally ill relative, for example, may be just as valuable and provide just as much insight as a medical ethicist's professional opinion. The editors have two additional purposes in including these less known views. One, the editors encourage readers to respect others' opinions—even when not enhanced by professional credibility. It is only by reading or listening to and objectively evaluating others' ideas that one can determine whether they are worthy of consideration. Two, the inclusion of such viewpoints encourages the important critical thinking skill of objectively evaluating an author's credentials and bias. This evaluation will illuminate an author's reasons for taking a particular stance on an issue and will aid in readers' evaluation of the author's ideas.

It is our hope that these books will give readers a deeper understanding of the issues debated and an appreciation of the complexity of even seemingly simple issues when good and honest people disagree. This awareness is particularly important in a democratic society such as ours in which people enter into public debate to determine the common good. Those with whom one disagrees should not be regarded as enemies but rather as people whose views deserve careful examination and may shed light on one's own.

Thomas Jefferson once said that "difference of opinion leads to inquiry, and inquiry to truth." Jefferson, a broadly educated man, argued that "if a nation expects to be ignorant and free . . . it expects what never was and never will be." As individuals and as a nation, it is imperative that we consider the opinions of others and examine them with skill and discernment. The Opposing Viewpoints Series is intended to help readers achieve this goal.

David L. Bender and Bruno Leone,
Founders

Introduction

"As headlines go, here's an attention-grabber: 'High schoolers lie, cheat, but say they're good.'"

Julie Muhlstein,
Everett (WA) Herald,
December 3, 2008

The Josephson Institute of Ethics gave almost thirty thousand high school students a failing grade in ethical conduct in its 2008 Report Card on the Ethics of American Youth. "[It] reveals entrenched habits of dishonesty in today's young people," the institute claims, "and that doesn't bode well for the future when these youngsters become the next generation's politicians and parents, cops and corporate executives, and journalists and generals."[1] For instance, the 2008 Report Card indicates that 35 percent of males and 26 percent of females said they had stolen an item from a store in the past year, up from 32 percent and 23 percent, respectively, in 2006. The numbers among honor students, student leaders, and those active in extracurricular activities were lower, but still exceeded 20 percent overall. The 2008 Report Card also showed that lying was prevalent; 49 percent of males and 36 percent of females admitted that they had lied to save money, up from 47 percent and 31 percent in 2006. Furthermore, 83 percent of both public and private school students revealed that they had lied to their parents about something important. And when it came to academic dishonesty, 64 percent of both sexes said they cheated on a test during the past year, jumping from 60 percent in 2006. In addition, 36 percent confessed to plagiarizing from the Internet in their schoolwork.

1. "Press Release: Josephson Institute Report Card on American Youth: There's a Hole in Our Moral Ozone and It's Getting Bigger," November 30, 2008. http://character counts.org/pdf/reportcard/2008/press-release.pdf.

Executive director Rich Jarc was shocked at the results. "It's pretty alarming and pretty scary," Jarc says. "The numbers are so high, I don't know how much worse it could get."[2] Arguably more compelling is how the respondents described themselves in the survey. "Despite these high levels of dishonesty, these same kids have a high self-image when it comes to ethics," the institute contends. "A whopping 93 percent said they were satisfied with their personal ethics and character, and 77 percent said that 'when it comes to doing what is right, I am better than most people I know.'"[3]

Commentators in agreement with Josephson Institute's findings were not surprised, however. "Instead of being rooted in an objective moral order that exists independently of ourselves, right and wrong are subjective—they're the product of the person's 'values,'" asserts Charles Colson, founder of the Prison Fellowship Ministries. "In that case, it makes perfect sense that people can lie, cheat, and steal and still be 'satisfied' with their ethics. After all, they are not answerable to God or the community, only to themselves."[4] Greg Laurie, senior pastor of the Harvest Christian Fellowship, contends that youths choose their values the way they listen to music on their iPods—they simply pick and choose what they want. "We truly have become the iGeneration," he declares. "We order our private universe and expect that the world will somehow revolve around us. The iGeneration even has its own morals, which we seem to make up as we go."[5]

Others, however, questioned the claims of the 2008 Report Card. Terry Mattingly, columnist for the Scripps Howard News Service, advises that the figures do not apply to every young

2. Quoted in Jennifer Eng, "More Students Admit to Cheating," *Boston University Daily Free Press*, December 9, 2008. www.dailyfreepress.com/more-students-admit-to-cheating-1.1096864.

3. "Press Release: Josephson Institute Report Card on American Youth."

4. "The Disturbing Ethics of America's Youth," Christian Broadcasting Network, 2008. www.cbn.com/family/parenting/colson_KidsEthics.aspx.

5. *WorldNetDaily*, December 13, 2008. www.wnd.com/index.php?fa=PAGE.view&pageId=83465.

person. "The problem with the Josephson Institute's latest survey ... is that it contained so many bad numbers that many readers were tempted to pin an 'all of the above' verdict on most teens," he states.[6] Also, Kathleen Kennedy Manzo, an associate editor for *Education Week*, proposes that the motivations behind the behaviors deserve a closer look. "The report doesn't give much insight into why, but could increasing testing pressure have something to do with it?" she asks. "Or perhaps teens see dishonesty in school as something entirely different from lying or cheating at home or at work."[7] And Stephen Lunn, a writer for the newspaper the *Australian*, suggests that the 2008 Report Card may not be fully objective: "The Josephson Institute does have some self-interest in highlighting this behaviour, given it runs a program called Character Counts, selling curriculum kits for teachers and advice books for parents on how to better develop their children."[8]

The 2008 Report Card adds to the robust debate of morality and values in the United States. From moral education in schools to the prospect of human cloning, *Opposing Viewpoints: Ethics* outlines these contemporary issues in the following chapters: Why Should People Behave Ethically? What Motivates People to Behave Ethically? Are Modern Biomedical Practices Ethical? Are Ethics in Business Practices Beneficial? The authors' pointed and conflicting opinions represent the religious, scientific, and philosophical sides of ethical inquiry in this thought-provoking volume.

6. Terry Mattingly, "Sobering Numbers on Teen Behavior," *Pocono Record*, December 19, 2008. www.poconorecord.com/apps/pbcs.dll/article?AID=/20081219/NEWS04/812190302

7. Kathleen Kennedy Manzo, "More Teens Lie, Cheat and Steal," edweek.org, December 1, 2008. http://blogs.edweek.org/edweek/curriculum/2008/12/more-teens-lie-cheat-and-steal.html

8. Stephen Lunn, "The Kids Are Not Alright," *Australian*, December 9, 2008. www.theaustralian.com.au/news/opinion/the-kids-are-not-all-right/story-e6frg71o-1111118257959

 OPPOSING
VIEWPOINTS®
SERIES

CHAPTER 1

Why Should People Behave Ethically?

Chapter Preface

On September 3, 2009, R&B star Chris Brown stated on *Larry King Live*, "I just feel like I just need to prove to people I can be a role model." Nine days earlier, he had been sentenced to five years of probation and six months of community service for committing felony assault against his ex-girlfriend, recording artist Rihanna, that February. "We're both young," Brown claimed. "Nobody taught us how to love one another. Nobody bought us a book on how to control our emotions or our anger."

Two months later, Rihanna broke her silence on the abuse in an interview on *20/20*. "This happened to me, and it could happen to anybody," she said. Rihanna also stated that she ended her relationship with Brown to set a better example for young women living with domestic violence. "When I realized that my selfish decision for love could result in some young girl getting killed, I could not be easy with that," she explained.

The scandal raised the issue of whether celebrities are role models. In March 2009, after Brown and Rihanna had reunited, writer Tina Kells argued, "Chris Brown and Rihanna had a shot at showing their fans how to overcome domestic violence in the most healthy and constructive way possible and in that they have failed. Their young and impressionable fans deserve better." Also, in reaction to a Rihanna interview in the December 2009 issue of *Glamour*, blogger Jessica Wakeman criticizes her soft stance on abusive relationships: "Wouldn't it have been awesome if she had said, 'Chris never should have hit me.' Or, 'If a man hits you, you need to leave immediately.' Or, 'People who love you don't hit you.'"

Dissenting commentators insist that neither Brown nor Rihanna need to set good examples for young people. Simon Vozick-Levison of *Entertainment Weekly* asserts that Rihanna does not have such an obligation: "She was the victim of a crime—that doesn't make it her responsibility to be a public advocate." Moreover, writer Mark Harris proposes, "Here's what they call the 'teachable moment': Don't hit women. And don't give men who hit you a chance to hit you again, ever. But if we really need Rihanna and Chris Brown, or any celebrities at all, to teach us that, we are in seriously bad shape." In the following chapter, the authors debate why people should behave ethically.

| "Our actions today . . . can have signifi-
cant effects over scores or even hundreds of generations."

People Should Behave Ethically for the Sake of Future Generations

Jonathan Gilligan

Jonathan Gilligan is a senior lecturer at Vanderbilt University's Department of Earth and Environmental Sciences. In the follow-ing viewpoint, Gilligan asserts that society has an ethical respon-sibility to future generations and the welfare of the planet. He states that decisions in handling hazardous waste, conserving natural resources, and addressing the human impact on climate and the environment will affect people thousands of years from now. Defining this ethical responsibility is complex, Gilligan con-tinues, and the different philosophical approaches have their strengths and flaws. Therefore, he offers that spiritual faith can provide guidance and reinforcement.

Jonathan Gilligan, "Ethics in Geologic Time: Should We Care About Distant Future Generations?" The Berry Lecture at Vanderbilt University, March 24, 2008. Reproduced by permission of the author.

As you read, consider the following questions:

1. According to the author, why is a contract between generations now and in the future problematic?

2. How are obligations to future generations diluted, in Gilligan's view?

3. As stated by the author, how is the idea of community important to survival?

Modern industry is producing large quantities of materials that are either directly hazardous because they are toxic or radioactive, or indirectly hazardous because they can change the environment in dangerous ways. Radioactive waste products from the nuclear weapons and nuclear energy programs will remain very dangerous for hundreds of thousands of years.

Carbon dioxide from burning fossil fuels currently remains in the air for 100–150 years, but if we go on burning fossil fuel until all the known coal reserves are depleted, the chemist James Kasting has calculated that it will take on the order of 2 million years for the atmosphere to recover. We may also be close to a point of climatic instability beyond which climate change will accelerate and become self-sustaining even if we cut further greenhouse gas emissions. A recent paper by [NASA scientist] James Hansen claims that we have already crossed such a tipping point, but that paper remains very controversial even among expert climate scientists. Even if we have not yet crossed this tipping point, if we do nothing to reduce fossil fuel use, it is possible, but not certain, that by 2100 global warming will have set one third of the world's plant and animal species on the path to extinction.

Apart from climate change, overfishing has depleted the population of one third of commerically fished species by 90% or more and has depleted the population of 90% of the fish species by at least half. In earth's past history, when mass extinctions have occurred it has taken many millions of years for biodiversity to recover, so we risk condemning thousands of generations to life in an impoverished ecosystem. Will there be insects to pollinate their crops? Will there be predators to keep pests that spread disease or spoil crops under control? What is the future of fishing, which is a vital part of many nations' food supply?

Our actions today in managing hazardous materials, husbanding natural resources, and interacting with the earth's climate and ecology, can have significant effects over scores or even hundreds of generations. At the same time, while many of these environmental threats may hurt us or our immediate descendants (children, grandchildren), many of these predominantly affect very distant generations.

Environmental concerns over the proposed nuclear waste repository at Yucca Mountain, Nevada, focus hazards to people living 10,000 to a few hundred thousand years in the future. Although the effects of global warming are becoming apparent as we speak, the kinds of catastrophic harm that could justify massive efforts to eliminate fossil fuel consumption are unlikely [to] arrive before the end of this century. While we fear the complete melting of the polar ice caps, which would cause an 80-foot sea-level rise that would put all of Florida, Louisiana and 40% of the continental U.S. under water, that may not happen; and if it does, even in the worst case it would not happen for several centuries. The threats are real, although uncertain, but because they will not materialize for so long a surprising number of scholars conclude that we do not owe our distant posterity very much consideration.

The distinguished economist Wilfred Beckerman dismissed obligations to future generations: "Suppose that, as a result of using up all the world's resources, human life did come to an end. So what? What is so desirable about an indefinite continuation of the human species, religious convictions apart?"

Can we take this moral sentiment seriously? I reject it and address myself to those who do likewise.

To many, the distance of those future generations diminishes their claim upon us. Out of sight is, if not out of mind, at least far from our attention. Where [philosopher David] Hume's comment that "'Tis not contrary to reason to prefer the destruction of the whole world to the scratching of my finger" is meant to reduce *a priori* ethics to absurdity, [philosopher] Adam Smith notes that a "man of humanity" would lose sleep over the prospect of losing his little finger tomorrow, but would sleep soundly after reading of the deaths of a hundred million Chinese in a distant earthquake. Consider, then, whether this same man would sacrifice those hundred millions to save his finger. "Human nature startles with horror at the thought," Smith writes, "and the world, in its greatest depravity and corruption, never produced such a villain as could be capable of entertaining it." The difference, according to Smith, between our "sordid and selfish" passive sentiments and our noble and generous actions is not reason, but conscience: "the love of what is honorable and noble."

There are many approaches to the ethics of posterity. I will consider three of these, and because of limited time, I will only be able to present the barest sketch of each and will fail to do justice to its strengths or to plausible responses to my arguments against them. I will address utilitarian, contractarian, and communitarian views of posterity. In so doing, I am walking largely in the footsteps of [political science professor] Avner de-Shalit, whose book *Why Posterity Matters* is one of the major contributions to intergenerational ethics.

Utilitarianism

The dominant school of utilitarian thought regarding environmental ethics focuses on economic wealth as a proxy for utility. If we can assume that economic wealth will grow exponentially without bound, then future generations will be incomprehensibly rich. If the world economy grows at a paltry 3% per year after inflation, the global average person living 1000 years from now will earn around 50 quadrillion dollars a year and thus will have so much disposable income that he or she will easily be able to clean up any mess our generations have left behind.

Of course, this same sort of logic applied to real estate prices led many people to make profligate use of home equity loans, and we should be cautious about assuming that the future will take care of itself.

Stemming global warming, safely disposing of nuclear waste, preserving habitats for wildlife, and reducing fish catches to sustainable levels all require real sacrifices today. Moreover, none of these matters is a binary decision. We can spend different amounts of money to purchase differing degrees of environmental security for the future.

There is also serious poverty and suffering today. [Danish scholar] Bjorn Lomborg and others see poverty and disease in the developing world as more serious and certain evils than the rather uncertain and temporally remote consequences of global warming. How, Lomborg asks, can we allow millions of children to die of malaria, AIDS, or starvation today in order to protect future generations from environmental hazards of uncertain magnitude?

This is a serious question, that deserves a more thorough response than I can give [at this time]. For now I will not address how to balance conflicting obligations to the future and to the present, but only ask whether we have *any* significant obligation to the distant future. Consider the role of uncertainty. As we imagine the effects of our actions on posterity, we become less and less confident with each succeeding generation what, if any, effect our actions today will have. We also become increasingly uncertain over what, apart from such basic necessities as life and health, future generations will value;

so in addition to not knowing the consequences of today's actions we are also ignorant of the value of those consequences.

Values are further complicated by a large and growing body of empirical psychological literature that clearly demonstrates that under conditions of anticipation and uncertainty, our preferences dramatically violate consistency and rationality, so the notion that utility is something we can measure consistently or objectively is questionable.

Utilitarian analysis can nonetheless attempt to account for our obligation to the future, but as the incendiary controversy over [economist] Nicholas Stern's economic analysis of the effects of global warming over the next several centuries demonstrates, compounding opportunity costs represent an almost insuperable barrier to any call for significant action on behalf of posterity.

For these reasons, utilitarian accounts of posterity tend to minimize our responsibility beyond a few generations. Some have attempted to rescue a subset of ethical obligation from a future that comprises both a fog of uncertainty and compounding opportunity costs by distinguishing those consequences that are qualitatively significant and irreversible from those that are merely quantitative or at least somewhat reversible. [Philosopher] Peter Singer writes,

> There are some things that, once lost, no amount of money can regain. Thus, to justify the loss of an ancient forest on the grounds that it will earn us substantial export income is unsound, even if we could invest that income and increase its value from year to year; for no matter how much we increased its value, it could never buy back the link with the past represented by the forest.

However, economists will point out that we make irreversible decisions all the time (look up "sunk costs" in any economics textbook) and markets for options provide rich data from which to infer the value we place on certainty and choice, at least over the short run. Thus, the desire to take irreversible harm to nature off the table appears arbitrary and subjective from a strictly utilitarian point of view and it becomes hard for utilitarianism to provide much guidance if we stubbornly persist in caring about the distant future.

Contractarianism

Perhaps the dominant deontological approach (meaning one that focuses on duties rather than consequences) to the problem of distant generations is rooted in the social contract. [Philosopher] Edmund Burke famously wrote:

> Society is indeed a contract. Subordinate contracts for objects of mere occasional interest may be dissolved at pleasure—but the state ought not to be considered as nothing better than a partnership agreement in a trade of pepper and coffee, calico, or tobacco, or some other such low concern, to be taken up for a little temporary interest, and to be dissolved by the fancy of the parties. . . . It is to be looked on with other reverence, because it is not a partnership in things subservient only to the gross animal existence of a temporary and perishable nature. It is a partnership in all science; a partnership in all art; a partnership in every virtue and in all perfection. As the ends of such a partnership cannot be obtained in many generations, it becomes a partnership not only between those who are living, but between those who are living, those who are dead, and those who are to be born.

However, the notion of an intergenerational contract between the dead, the living, and the unborn raises many difficulties. A contract is an agreement negotiated amongst its parties and voluntarily subscribed. The social contract is a fiction that binds everyone at birth to the extent that entering into it is preferable to remaining in some hypothetical state of nature. It is a small, though not negligible, exercise of imagination to picture ourselves negotiating such a contract with the current generations of humanity.

It is a much greater task to imagine how such a negotiation would proceed between our generations and all those that will come during the next millennium. The notion of negotiating from a state of ignorance as to which millennium one will inhabit defeats [philosopher John] Rawls's "original position" and reduces his concern for future generations to the few that immediately succeed the present, with care for the distant future reduced to a principle of "just savings." by which successive generations hold some share of resources in trust.

To the contractarian, we do not know what the future will desire, we cannot negotiate with the future, and the future can neither reciprocate our consideration nor retaliate against our neglect. [Economist] Robert Heilbroner points out that a contractarian might ask, "What has posterity ever done for me?" Without the possibility of reciprocity and sanctions, the metaphor of a social contract falls apart and we must look elsewhere for guidance on our obligations toward the future.

Our colleagues at law will not hesitate to remind us that a contract is meaningless without a means of enforcing it. But next century, much less next millennium, cannot enforce a contract against us. We might cobble together a notion of reciprocity through the duty of remembrance as future generations' payment for our faithful stewardship, but neither we nor posterity has any real means of enforcing the deal, so speaking of this arrangement as a binding social contract stretches the metaphor.

If our intuitive sympathies impose an obligation toward the future, contractarian thinking will not help clarify our thoughts and match actions to our ends.

Communitarianism

Avner de-Shalit and [philosopher] Avishai Margalit, present communitarian views of our relation to posterity. Both situate ethical obligation within a community. Margalit draws a care-

Our Genetic Interests

In order for our genes to successfully be passed on, it is necessary that our behavior not get in the way. This means somehow motivating us to ensure that our genes have a hospitable future to grow into, to have offspring, and to care for those offspring enough to give them a good start. The motivation to have offspring is well covered by making sex such a pleasurable experience. The other motivations take the form of felt moral obligations, both serving our genetic interests. It is therefore not surprising that they would resemble each other. The correlation is even made for us in public appeals for conservation policies that take the form of saving the future for your children, and their children. This kind of appeal is made quite frequently, though philosophers have seemed slow to pick up on it.

Norman R. Schultz,
"But What Has Posterity Ever Done for Me?
Concern for Future Generations and the Selfish Gene,"
www.normanrschultz.org.

ful distinction between ethics, which operates within a community and treats each member of that community as a valued and respected individual, and morals, which operate outside of the community and describe our obligations toward humanity in general. *Morals*, to Margalit, are more universal and impersonal, while *ethics* are personal and individual. Margalit identifies a crucial difference between two strains of thought that he labels "Jewish" and "Christian:" Scripture tells us to love our neighbor as ourself, but who is a neighbor? Jews maintain a clear boundary between the Jewish community (neighbors) and the rest of humanity and Christians seek to extend the neighborhood of the ethical to all humanity. The parable of the good Samaritan exemplifies this difference and the Christian perspective is beautifully set forth by [civil rights leader] Martin Luther King Jr., in a 1956 sermon:

> America, . . . I wonder whether your moral and spiritual progress has been commensurate with your scientific progress. It seems to me that your moral progress lags behind your scientific progress. Your poet [Henry David] Thoreau used to talk about "improved means to an unimproved end." How often this is true. You have allowed the material means by which you live to outdistance the spiritual ends for which you live. You have allowed your mentality to outrun your morality. You have allowed your civilization to outdistance your culture. Through your scientific genius you have made of the world a neighborhood, but through your moral and spiritual genius you have failed to make of it a brotherhood.

Scripture commands that we love our neighbor as ourself. Margalit tells us that to the Jew, the neighbor is any other Jew, while Christ preached of Samaritans and Jews being neighbors.

In what follows, I will use Margalit's terminology, but it is important to stress that these labels are shorthand, and do not necessarily apply only to Christians or Jews, nor universally to all Christians and all Jews. Moreover, the attitudes so labeled do not necessarily entail religious belief, but may arise simply from membership in a community that shares those values.

De-Shalit seeks to overcome the problems whereby neither utilitarians nor contractarians can produce a compelling explanation of our obligations to generations who will be born more than a short time after our own deaths. To de-Shalit, the notion of a community that endures over time provides an ethical fabric that connects us to those we will not know, but who share enough of our values and who will be tied closely enough to us through a web of overlapping relationships that we can meaningfully care for them as we care for our neighbors.

However, as we look farther and farther into the future, we know less and less of our descendants' values and are likely to have less and less in common with them. To de-Shalit, this dilutes our obligation, so that although we have clear duties to the generations that will come over the next several generations, the connection is diluted over time and it is almost inconceivable that we would share many values in common with those born millennia in the future:

> We should therefore accept the principle that we should sacrifice something (how much and what is a separate question) for the sake of remote future generations. At the same time, it is unreasonable to think in terms of sharing control over goods with people who will live two thousand years from now.

In describing the ebbing of responsibility while denying that we can ever completely stop caring for future generations, de-Shalit distinguishes justice, which we owe to people within our own community, from *humane consideration*, which we owe to all people throughout time.

> It is arguable that we cannot and should not allow every needy person [to] join our community. . . . All the same, we should not be indifferent to their plight.

This mirrors Margalit's distinction between ethics within a community and morals throughout humankind.

Exclusion from the community has a different role for the two: to de-Shalit, exclusion is a matter of survival. The community has only so much food to go around so if you start admitting every beggar to an equal share the whole community will go hungry. To Margalit, exclusion is a more spiritual matter. The community can only have a shared purpose if this purpose distinguishes it from other communities, so even in a world of plenty the community must have a boundary to define its purpose. To Margalit, this *intratemporal* boundary serves an important *intertemporal* purpose. If part of the religious life of the community is preserving the memories of those who have left the mortal coil, consider that everyone in the generation born 300 years from now will have roughly 1000 ancestors from our generation to keep track of. That is too many stories and names to remember. And the generation born 1000 years hence will have billions of names and stories to maintain. To Margalit, membership in a community with a definite purpose can keep our stories alive even as our individuality fades from memory in the multiplicity of generations. To the extent that we participated in the common project, we have an identity within the intergenerational community even as our personal thread fades into the larger tapestry.

What Is to Be Done?

I propose that the Christian turn of making all humanity neighbors is compatible with a shared purpose in caring for creation. This need not necessarily mean literal acceptance of Christ, but uses *Christian* in Margalit's sense to label an attitude commonly associated with Christian values.

The problem with this endeavor is whether it is in any way practical to extend the realm of community to embrace not just people living today but the billions who will follow us through time. My thoughts on this are less developed and represent a somewhat literal leap of faith. [Law professor] Roberto Mangabeira Unger described communities, or "organic groups" as incomplete realizations of an ideal toward which we strive. "There are necessarily limits to our capacity to achieve in the world natural harmony, sympathy, and concrete universality."

> When philosophy has gained the truth of which it is capable, it passes into politics and prayer, politics through

which the world is changed, prayer through which men ask God to complete the change of the world by carrying them into His presence and giving them what, left to themselves, they would always lack.

This role of faith in completing the moral community resonates with the great meteorologist Sir John Houghton's account of environmental responsibility:

In facing environmental problems ... we are called to exercise stewardship in as thorough a manner as possible, looking to God for the ability to carry it out. For any situation there are bound to be limitations to our knowledge and our ability to control; what we are invited to do is to go into the situation in partnership with God, knowing that he can take care of those things which we cannot.

This faith may be literal religious faith in God's voice and God's hand in our lives, or it may take the form of a less direct spiritual experience, but as the gap between our generation and those of the fourth millennium and onward is too great for our moral reason to span, a non-rational spiritual element is necessary if we are to preserve more than a nominal moral obligation to the distant future.

| "Our responsibility is to do God's will ourselves and to proclaim in word and action to the rest of the world what God expects of his creatures who bear his image."

People Should Behave Ethically Because It Is God's Will

Kenneth Boa

In the following viewpoint, Kenneth Boa contends that biblical ethics are universally relevant and should be followed by both Christians and non-Christians. He maintains that the teachings of the Bible apply to contemporary society because they contain unchanging standards of morality that reflect God's holiness and goodness. Also, Boa tasks Christians with modeling and pro-claiming God's will to others. In a society of religious pluralism, Christians must show that their ethical beliefs—which are found in other religions—are right for everyone, he insists. The author is president of Reflections Ministries and Trinity House Publish-ers and is an evangelistic speaker.

Kenneth Boa, "Ethics as If God Mattered: Secularism and the Word of God," bible.org, March 27, 2006. Reproduced by permission.

As you read, consider the following questions:

1. What are the arguments against biblical ethics, as stated by the author?

2. What are effects of secularization on society, according to Boa?

3. In the author's view, why do Christians have "dual citizenship"?

"What is the meaning of existence? ... Man and woman persons, their existence means exactly and precisely, not more, not one tiny bit less, just what they think it means, and what I think doesn't count at all."

—*"God" (George Burns), in Oh, God (1977)*

We have argued that there are moral absolutes, and that it is on the basis of the transcendent authority of Jesus Christ over all cultures that we conclude that those moral absolutes are to be found in Scripture. But this conclusion is widely questioned today, even by Christians. In this [viewpoint], we will consider two basic objections to treating biblical morality as absolute.

First, it is often alleged that biblical morality applied only to people *in the past*. The moral teachings of the Bible may have been fine and helpful for people thousands of years ago, it is often urged, but they can hardly be regarded as binding on us today.

Second, it is also often argued that biblical morality applies only to people *in the church* (and not necessarily even all of them). That is, when it is admitted that the moral teachings of the Bible might have some contemporary relevance today, it is commonly suggested that its moral relevance is limited to those who profess to be Christians and who accept the Bible as their moral guide. The general point here is that anyone who *wants* to follow the Bible as their moral standard is, of course, free to do so, but those who do not choose to view the Bible in that way are free to follow another path.

The effect of both of these ideas, especially the latter, has been that Western civilization has become *secularized*. That is, while most people in the Western world recognize a legitimate place for commitment to God, such religious expression has been systematically excluded from public life. Not only are distinctive religious beliefs peculiar to certain denominations or religions held to be irrelevant to the social and political issues of our cities, states, and nations, but even the affirmation of our status as creatures responsible to our Creator is widely thought to be irrelevant. We have become a civilization in which one's belief or lack of belief in God is supposed to be irrelevant to the ethical questions facing us as a society. In short, we have come to the point of acting as a society as if it doesn't matter whether there is a God or not, or whether he approves of what we do or not.

Is biblical morality a relic from the past? Is it a code of conduct for Christians only? We will discuss both of these objections to the universal relevance of biblical morality in turn.

Is Biblical Morality for Today?

The Bible is now about two thousand years old. Because of its antiquity, many people today question the applicability of the Bible's moral teachings to contemporary life. Even many Christians today are less than fully confident in the relevance of the Bible to the problems and issues of modern society.

We need, then, to be very clear about *why* we regard the Bible as a reliable and authoritative standard for morality. It is not because it happens to be the source of moral values with which we were raised, or which has dominated Western civilization for so long. Such reasons would base our confidence in the Bible as a perfect and unchanging standard on our very imperfect and changing experiences and histories. To put it simply, we rely on the Bible as our standard for morality be-

cause we are convinced that its moral teachings come from *God*. While the point here may seem obvious, it is worth reflecting on its significance.

For Best Results, Follow the Directions

First of all, the God of the Bible is *the God who made the world and humanity* (Gen. 1–2; Ex. 20:8–11; Acts 17:24–28), and whose instructions to humanity must therefore be obeyed. If God made us, he has every right to tell us how to live. Indeed, by creating the world in which we live and designing us to live in this world in relationships with one another, he determined for us what is right and wrong. The Bible simply reminds us or explains to us how God made and designed us and what behaviors are consistent with God's creation and what behaviors are not. In other words, in the Bible we find a perfectly reliable reminder in human words of the universal, natural moral law.

Second, the God who gave us the Bible *proved himself to be the true God*. The God of the Bible is not a symbol for the moral ideal, or a mythological figure, or the projection of an ideal father figure. This is a God who speaks and acts. This is the God who spoke to Abraham, Isaac, and Jacob, who spoke to Israel through Moses and the prophets, and who spoke to us definitively and personally in his Son, Jesus Christ (Heb. 1:1–2). This is the God who proved himself to be the God of the whole earth by his miraculous deliverance of the Israelites out of Egypt (Ex. 19:4–5; 20:2–3; Deut. 4:32–40; etc.). This is the God who proved himself to be the true God, the God of life, by raising Jesus from the dead (Acts 17:30–31). This is not a God who tells us what to do but does nothing himself, but a God who has done what no other religion has even dared to claim.

Third, the moral standards given to us in the Bible are the true standards of what is good because God *is perfectly good and does only good*. Everything God created was created perfectly good (Gen. 1:4, 10, 12, 18, 21, 25, 31). Everything God says and does is right (Gen. 19:25; Deut. 32:4). This means that God never requires from us anything but good. Moreover, what God intends for our lives is good. Even things which happen to us that are bad can and will be used by God for our good if we trust in his goodness (Gen. 50:20; Rom. 8:28).

Fourth, the Bible is accepted as the supreme written standard of morality because God *determined that the moral teachings of the Bible would reflect his own holy character* (Lev. 19:2; Rom. 7:12; 1 Pet. 1:14–16). The moral standards of the Bible are not arbitrary rules designed merely to test our fortitude, patience, or loyalty to God. They are expressions of God's own perfectly good, perfectly holy moral character. What God tells us to do is a reflection of what God is like and what God does. This is what we would expect if we were made in God's image, as the Bible tells us (Gen. 1:26–27). This brings us back to our first reason for trusting in the moral standards of the Bible—they come from our Creator.

Finally, the morality of the Bible is applicable to us today because the God of the Bible *is unchangingly good and faithfully consistent* (Deut. 7:9; Ps. 136; Mal. 3:6; Heb. 13:8). God's purpose and standards do not vacillate or change. Because he is dependably, unchangeably good, we know that what he laid down for his people two and even three thousand years ago still applies today. Since God does not change at all, and since human nature has not changed (even if our circumstances have), what God reveals in Scripture as his standards for human life and relationships is as relevant to us today as it was to Abraham, Moses, Amos, and Paul.

Numerous objections to the Christian view of the Bible as revealing unchanging moral standards have, of course, been put forth. We will consider some of these objections. But it should be pointed out to those who would dispute it that simply citing supposed "difficulties" with this view of the Bible is not enough. Those who would deny the Bible's *moral* truth—what it says about life and death, sex and money—must first explain why they reject its *historical* truth—what it says about Abraham and Moses, David and Christ. In other words, it makes no sense to deny the moral authority of the Bible while refusing to consider the evidence for the divine origin of the Bible. . . .

Is Biblical Morality for Everyone?

Many Christians, of course, do agree that those of us who believe in the Bible as the word of God should live by its moral teachings. But even when this fact is recognized, and the absolute character of biblical morality is appreciated, the relevance of the Bible to the moral issues facing our society today is often questioned. Even if we as Christians live by the precepts of the Bible, can we really expect non-Christians to do so? It is widely believed that we cannot and should not expect non-

Christians to live by the moral standards of Scripture. As many see it, the Bible belongs in the church, but not in the Congress; its values should be promoted in our Sunday schools, but not in our public schools.

The implications of this view of Scripture for Christian involvement in the issues of the society in which they live are far-reaching. It implies that if Christians come to certain moral convictions about such matters as abortion, divorce, euthanasia, and homosexuality on the basis of their study of the Bible, they are free to hold those views—but they have no business trying to make those views normative for the whole of society. What shall we say to those who question the relevance of biblical morality to the issues of our day?

The Prophetic Stance

First of all, we have already seen that the nature of the Bible as a revelation from the Creator of the entire human race militates against the idea that biblical morality does not apply to all people. The law which God gave to Israel was not a set of arbitrary rules, but an expression of the goodness, holiness, and justice of God.

Moreover, the ethical teaching of Jesus and his disciples was not merely for their hearers only, but for people of all nations. Jesus told his disciples to make disciples *of all nations*, teaching them to *observe everything he had taught.* (Matt. 28:19–20). It is true that here Jesus implies that full and voluntary submission to his moral teaching will be expected only of disciples. But at the same time it is clear that Jesus authoritatively calls upon all people of all nations to submit to his teaching. That is why Jesus prefaced his command to make disciples with the observation that "all authority" had been given to him "in heaven and on earth" (v. 18). Thus, people who refuse to become disciples, who refuse to observe all that Christ commanded, are in rebellion against the sovereign King of the universe, the one who has authority over it all.

From one perspective, then, while it is quite true to say that non-Christians cannot be counted on to observe the moral standards of Scripture, that does not change the fact that all people *ought* to observe those standards. This is just another way of saying that all people ought to do God's will. We are all accountable to God for how we live, and will have to answer to him for our lives, whether we called ourselves Christians or not.

The Christian task from this perspective is a *prophetic* one. Our responsibility is to do God's will ourselves and to proclaim in word and action to the rest of the world what God expects of his creatures who bear his image. We do this, not merely as individuals, but as families and churches, modeling what institutions based on those moral principles should look like, and encouraging others to do likewise. We know that God's will is ultimately about having a relationship with God based on love and trust, and so we not only model and proclaim God's moral standards, but we also model and proclaim the gospel of reconciliation to the Father through faith in his Son Jesus Christ. This prophetic stance of proclamation is carried out in the awareness that we have a citizenship which is from heaven (Phil. 3:20–21)—membership in an eternal community of the redeemed who will enjoy life in the new heavens and new earth in which God's moral standards are perfectly realized (2 Pet. 3:13).

The Public Stance

It is sometimes thought that the prophetic task of modeling and proclaiming the moral standards of God's heavenly kingdom is inconsistent with involvement in social and political issues. But this is not so. Christians have a kind of "dual citizenship," with a responsibility both to God's eternal, heavenly kingdom and to the temporal, earthly governments of the nations of which they are a part (cf. Rom. 13:1–10; 1 Tim. 2:1–4; 1 Pet. 2:9–17). This is similar to our family situation: We are members of God's heavenly, supernatural family (the church) while remaining members of our earthly, natural families. Just as we can advance the interests of our eternal family by participating faithfully in our temporal families, we can advance the interests of God's heavenly kingdom by participating faithfully in the affairs of our earthly nations. In doing so, we will be able to show that God's moral standards are relevant and applicable to all areas of life, including politics.

Thus, involvement in public life and public affairs is a natural extension of our prophetic stance. It is not an either/or proposition, but both/and: our effort to promote justice and righteousness in society goes hand in hand with our effort to proclaim God's message of judgment and reconciliation. We cannot expect to show that God's will is relevant to all people in all areas of their life if we do not show that God's will is relevant to the most entrenched problems and controversial issues of our day.

In working for justice and moral standards in society, we will of course be approaching the issues from the perspective of our biblical, Christian moral convictions. But this does not mean that when we are engaged in controversy in public affairs with people who do not share our Christian commitment we will be able to appeal only to the Bible and its authoritative teaching. It is not necessary to quote Scripture or to assume its authority to promote biblical moral standards. To some extent this is obvious. All societies agree in general that it is immoral to commit murder, to steal private property, to commit perjury in a court of law, and so forth. We do not need to convince a whole nation to believe in the Bible before we can urge that nation to enact laws that protect citizens from murder, theft, and false accusations.

We may go further still. We said earlier that in principle every rule that God laid down in Scripture governing human relationships reflects an unchanging moral truth. The moral truths, or principles, which are embodied and illustrated in the Bible are absolutes that are true for all people because they are the truth of what it means to be human beings in relationship with one another. That is, the moral standards of the Bible are a reminder to us of what we already know, or at least should know, is right and wrong. And this means that in principle it should be possible to understand and articulate the rationale or reason for every moral teaching and rule found in the Bible. In other words, we ought to be able to explain to non-Christians *why* certain things are wrong, or why other behaviors are morally right, without our explanation amounting to nothing more than "because the Bible says so." We ought to be able to show them that the moral standards we embrace are right for all people whether they are Christians or not.

In making a reasoned case for these moral standards, Christians will have to appeal implicitly to certain truths about God and human nature. The belief that all human beings at whatever stage of development are persons deserving of respect really assumes that human beings are not mere animals but are creatures endowed with a capacity or potential for relationship with God that distinguishes them among all living things. (Many atheists admit that all human beings should be given respect, but they have no rational basis for insisting on such a standard as a matter of public policy.) Traditional Christian beliefs about sexuality likewise assume that sexual intimacy is not merely a biological function (though it obviously includes such a function) but for human beings has a higher purpose ordained by the Creator. It will not be possible to make a complete case for Christian convictions about such moral issues without acknowledging that these convictions ultimately assume that we are created by a God who has in the act of creating us determined the purpose and design for our lives. Any moral system that is not based on that premise must ultimately allow human beings to determine their own purposes, if any, and to make whatever choices they wish.

Still, in developing their case for a public morality that agrees with the moral standards revealed in Scripture, Christians will not have to appeal to uniquely Christian beliefs. For example, most if not everything that has just been said about God and human nature in relation to ethics can be and is affirmed by many Jews and Muslims. The arguments Christians put forth in debates about culture and public life will be *informed* by Scripture; that is where we will go to check our values and to make sure that our moral judgments are in accord with what God has revealed to us. But then the arguments which we put forth will not be based on Scripture, but on truths about God and ourselves that are generally understood and acknowledged even outside of the Christian church.

In our religiously pluralistic society, then, the source of our moral convictions as Christians should be the word of God which has been uniquely revealed in Scripture. The way we express and defend those moral convictions in public life should be by appealing to the moral truths which are revealed to all human beings in their conscience and which have been admitted in most or all cultures.

| *"For ethics to be ethics, it must . . . bring rational order to our lives."*

People Should Behave Ethically Because It Is Reasonable to Do So

James Leroy Wilson

In the following viewpoint, James Leroy Wilson asserts that human decision and action must be based on reason to establish order and ethical behavior. He contends that reason is not derived from what is arbitrarily "good" or "ideal," but what is self-evident—it is the recognition of objects, structure, and patterns that bring order to existence. Consequently, the author states that reason should be used to explain human behavior and determine conduct before ideology, statistics, religion, or tradition. James Leroy Wilson is a Chicago-based columnist for the Partial Observer *and author of* Ron Paul Is a Nut (and So Am I).

As you read, consider the following questions:

1. How does the author respond to the argument that people have a basic right to health care, food, and shelter?

James Leroy Wilson, "My Debt to Mises," LewRockwell.com, May 24, 2004. Reproduced by permission of the publisher and author.

2. According to Wilson, what did Ludwig von Mises establish?

3. How does the author view the power of politics?

Even people who hate math actually love it. They depend on it, and they have faith in it. The only moral truth that everyone agrees on is that "2 + 2 = 4."

Why do I say that this is a "moral" truth? Because it brings order to our lives. That almost every non-mentally handicapped person knows the simple rules of addition and subtraction goes a long way toward explaining how civil society functions. The essential function of a store clerk is to count the money received and give exact change back, and it's normally not a difficult thing to do.

Nature, too, imposes order. Jumping off cliffs or tall buildings can normally be called suicide, and it is understood that humans can't fly. The belief that people "ought" to fly does not make it so; instead, one must find ways to fly that accord with the laws of nature. Humans fly, thanks to airplanes, helicopters, balloons, and some other contraptions. But these inventions work precisely because they conform to the laws of nature and physics. Wishing something to happen doesn't make it happen. Feeling that something ought to be right, doesn't make it right.

A Real, Ordered Natural World

In other words, we live in a real, ordered natural world, not of our own choosing. And it's actually the world we really want, precisely because it is ordered. Anyone who wants a world in which 2+2 can equal 5 whenever it's convenient, is essentially asking for the world to go to hell. To willfully believe such a thing is to negate one's own rational faculties, which itself is a negation of one's own desire for life and happiness.

I say that, fully aware that mathematics, the indispensable tool for the natural scientist, is itself an "a priori" science—

based on reason, not facts. By that, I mean, no two seemingly similar objects in the universe are ever, as a matter of empirical fact, "exactly" alike. No two eggs, no two apples, no two humans, no two clones. No naturally-appearing or human-built object has ever had an exact right angle, or has been perfectly spherical. The study of mathematics is the study of an ideal, or perhaps we should say, abstract, universe, which only means that reason itself recognizes the abstracts, the patterns—as opposed to the absolutes—of our actual universe. It is only through abstract reasoning, through logic, that we can actually see the order within the "real" universe.

Even in some intellectual struggles between "science" and "religion," the Creationists and other anti-Darwinists try to use logic and evidence to make their case; it is not just "the Bible tells me so." The argument has to make sense according to reason. The Cal-Berkeley law professor Philip Johnson, for one, has carved out a whole new career questioning the logic and evidence of Darwinism.

Curiously, however, reason isn't held in much regard in the field of ethics or the social sciences. For the most part, social scientists defer to history, statistics, conventional wisdom, and ideology to understand the premises, and then only use "reason" to reach the conclusions. The purpose of social science often seems to be to find data to prove ethical and ideological points. Pick the best arguments of your favorite economist, statistician, sociologist, and historian, and your ideology may appear to be quite rational.

Historical or empirical "evidence" are only data. Reason must explain the data; the data doesn't determine the conclusion. If we do that, then future behavior becomes a guessing game: when does "history" prove that war is "good for the economy" and when doesn't it; when does deficit spending bring on excessive inflation and when doesn't it. What "lessons" of history should we apply to future judgments?

That creates random judgments based on generalizations. Hey, we rebuilt Japan and Germany, why can't we do the same in Iraq? Words like "appeasement" haunt American politicians, who then exaggerate the magnitude of foreign "threats" to American "security interests." History may provide some patterns, but the job of the social scientist is to explain the pattern, and not assume that the pattern is itself the explanation.

The role of the social scientist in the political arena is to provide politicians with explanations of social, economic, and political phenomena. It is not to give politicians data from which they can "predict" the outcomes of a course of political action.

A Guessing Game

If political action, and by extension, all human action and ethics, is to be based on predictions of outcomes, then ethics does indeed become relative: everyone doing what is right in their own eyes. Ethics would become a guessing game, on the political and personal level, on whether the benefits outweigh the costs and risks. But if ethical rules are random, and if ethical conduct is arbitrary, then ethics doesn't really exist at all. There would be neither rhyme nor reason in the pursuit of happiness or of "the good." It is akin to wishing for the natural order to permit $2 + 2 = 5$, as stated above.

Many believe that democratic institutions provide a check on this randomness; the moral preferences of the majority prevail. But this doesn't prove that the majority's preferences are based on reason. Majority rule is still arbitrary rule.

Yet this randomness, this declaration of ethical "norms" by appealing to the desires of the majority, is all over the place. Think of this statement: "Health care is a basic human right." That is, it is an inherent right of an individual that some other individuals know how to practice medicine, and be forced to use their skills for free. Are food, clothing, and shelter also basic rights? If health care is, these must be, too. But also of course, someone must know how to grow the crops, kill and butcher the animal, produce the garments, and build the houses, and do this either for free or at fixed prices he can't control. One person's "rights" require forced labor from others. Economic "rights" are essentially the rights of the chattel slave—being forced into work not of your choice or even best ability, but in return you are "cared for." It is safe to say, that if our rights were based on economic sustenance, they can not co-exist with the rights expressed in our Bill of Rights—which guarantee not your own well-being but that you have the right be left alone, to be free.

(This, by the way, is the myth of modern liberalism, that the productive capacity of highly regulated and highly taxed markets in the modern age can make possible both economic "rights" and individual freedom, forever. But the record of the modern liberal, from Waco [a 1993 confrontation between federal agents and the Branch Davidian religious sect at the group's compound in Waco, Texas, resulting in the deaths of about eighty sect members] to McCain-Feingold [a 2002 campaign finance reform bill that banned "soft money" contributions], proves otherwise; the liberal will sacrifice the freedom of the individual for larger social and economic goals.)

Universal Truth?

What ethics frequently does, is inherit pre-conceived religious and political doctrines, combine them, and pass them off as universal truth. Hence the supposed split between what passes for "liberalism" and "conservatism" today. Liberals seek individual freedom provided there are economic guarantees; conservatives want a strong State and a free market, but only prefer the free market because it has traditionally worked, and has no idea of how or why it works. The inability of morally concerned clergy to competently "speak truth to power" whenever they recognize a grave evil is that they have abandoned, or never really had, the rational faculty to tell the truth. All they have, instead, is their moral beliefs based entirely on religious faith. These beliefs may be true, in a cosmic, spiritual, and religious sense, or may be not. But they lack the logic, the reason, which is our only guide to discern and articulate the truth.

In other words, social science and ethics, to be effective, must insist on abstract, logical thinking, just as mathematics plays that role in the natural sciences. This is not utopian analysis of envisioning the "good society" or the "moral human being" and deriving principles from them. It does not insist on exactitude in the real world.

Reason, instead, is derived from self-evident axioms. No two snowflakes, or dogs, or apples, or homes, or human beings are exactly alike, and mathematics does not urge that they ought to be so. But we must recognize an apple as an apple, if we are to count how many apples we have. By "self-evident axioms," I'm only suggesting that an apple of a different color is still an apple, and that an orange is not an apple. Mathematics is based on our recognition of the real world; our rational faculty is based on recognition of objects and the recognition of structure and patterns. It doesn't tell us what ought to be or what is "perfect" or "ideal," but in telling us the patterns and structure of what is, it does something better: it brings order to our lives.

Bringing Rational Order

For ethics to be ethics, it must do the same thing: bring rational order to our lives. Which means explaining how human action really works, the raw reasoning we need before we let ideology, religion, or tradition determine our conduct. Furthermore, it must not create theories out of raw historical data, it must rather, use reason to explain the historical data. Like mathematics, it must provide rules to be heeded for an ordered universe.

A Subdomain of Practical Reason

What ought I to do, how ought I to live? These are the central questions of moral thought; explaining the questions, and delimiting the range of acceptable answers, the tasks of moral philosophy. If so, the connection between morality and practical reason is already a close one: if one reads 'ought'-remarks, as many people do, as remarks about reason, then our questions are questions about what one has reason to do, and call directly for a theory of practical reason. On this view, morality is a subdomain of practical reason.

Garrett Cullity and Berys Nigel Gaut, eds.,
Ethics and Practical Reason, *1997.*

And in ethics and social science as a whole, it is the logic of human action itself, as opposed to finding the quirks of this or that individual or the beliefs of this or that population, that ultimately explains social phenomena. Not how many of what race voted for whom; not how a nation's Gross Domestic Product rose because of tax cuts (or tax hikes). Or rose, or fell, on account of war. The relationship of two or more sets of statistical data does not prove or disprove anything. We must use reason to understand what's really going on.

And this is the ultimate, supreme debt we owe to [philosopher and economist] Ludwig von Mises. He established, in *Human Action*, the premises and logic of human behavior. Not that human behavior is moral, or even reflects "rational self-interest." But rather, that human beings act by making choices through time, and that these choices are a reflection of costs and benefits according to one's values at the time of his decision and action. Just as green apples, red apples, and rotten apples are all still apples, it is self-evident—a rational discernment of recognition—that a human being makes choices through time. And that a human being's will is self-governing—that is, one person can influence, but not control, another person's will. An organism's will, and, as [libertarian writer] Rose Wilder Lane put it, "control of his own energy" is entirely up to the organism. Politics can influence us by imposing additional costs on certain behaviors, and provide rewards for others. But politics cannot control behavior or control values. In establishing these axioms, Mises systematically destroyed the conceit of the State, that its laws and coercion can function as values that can persuade people to become "good" in the State's eyes. Instead, he advanced the idea that the State only imposes additional costs and impediments on human action and thereby distorts it and takes away the freedom and prosperity we otherwise would have had.

Praxeology

Mises's greatest achievement was the very concept of "praxeology," the a priori science of human action. Praxeology is to social science what mathematics is to natural science: just as mathematical theorems explain natural data, so does praxeology explain human behavior—of human action as constituting choices through time. Physical evidence does not change mathematical analysis, nor could it. Likewise, social change does not alter praxeology. It is praxeology that explains the social change.

This is important. Mathematics not only best explains natural phenomena, it [is] the tool of technology, telling architects and engineers what can and can't be built. The slightest miscalculation in physics can cause an entire bridge to collapse. Mathematical precision is crucial to technological advancement. Mathematical equations describe the "order" of nature so as to make understanding it, and subduing it with technology, even possible.

Likewise, praxeology performs the same vital function in the social sciences and ethics. By describing the nature of human action, it reveals the order that is often hidden in the social world. It provides the social scientist the means to explain the statistical data, and it informs ideologues and ethicists that their dreams of a better society cannot emerge if they desire to subvert the deductions of praxeology in the process.

That's because the human being is an independent source of energy, with an independent will, and merely "complying" with the State's demands, which is avoiding punishment, is not the same as advancing the State's ends. Doing as little as possible in obedience to the State, is not the same as advancing the State's goals. The more the State imposes, the more costs are burdened on the people, the more the people will do as little in compliance to get by and become "outlaws" to improve their condition. Civilization crumbles, and with it, the State. Mises predicted this of communism in 1922 with his book *Socialism*. It also explains our crumbling moral fabric today. It will always be so when the people's individual desires and goals are not the same as those of the people who control the State.

Mises saw the logic—the order—of human action. It is to the extent that people were free, as opposed to being burdened by the demands and taxes of their authorities, that civilization flourished. And that is his lesson for us today. The less powerful, and less centralized, the government, the better. Because that leaves us with more freedom, with more initiative, to improve ourselves and society as a whole.

To desire another world, in which people are "good" or "virtuous" to your satisfaction and convenience, is like desiring that $2 + 2$ should equal 5. When counting your own money, that might seem like an alluring fantasy, but deep down, nobody wants to live in that world.

And that is my debt to Mises. He provided substance and reason to a value I already held dear: liberty.

"*What kids see and believe, they become. Each and every day, parents build a legacy for kids to inherit.*"

Adults Should Behave Ethically to Be Good Role Models for Children

Karen Stephens

Karen Stephens is director of Illinois State University (ISU) Child Care Center and teaches child development at the ISU Department of Family and Consumer Sciences. In the following viewpoint, Stephens maintains that leading by example is a powerful way for parents to teach their children ethical behavior and values. While some traits and characteristics may be passed on genetically, youngsters, the author claims, tend to mimic adults around them. Thus, Stephens advises that parents show self-discipline and accountability for their actions because children are sensitive to the credibility and hypocrisy of their role models.

As you read, consider the following questions:

1. How does the author compare the conventional wisdom of child rearing to what research has established?

2. What environmental factors can influence impulse control in children, as stated by Stephens?

3. What does the author challenge parents to identify?

"A chip off the old block." "Flip side of the same coin." "The apple doesn't fall far from the tree." "Like father, like son." "She lives up to the family name." "Trouble follows the footsteps of all those Hatfields (or McCoys—take your pick of any family in disfavor)." These folk phrases succinctly sum up family characterizations—some complimentary, others definitely not. They all [imply] that parents are to blame for how kids turn out—for better or worse.

Like quite a bit of other home-grown knowledge, these beliefs have, to a degree, been confirmed by researchers. Children, in general, do tend to grow up to be a lot like their parents. Social scientists and genetic researchers have identified many cycles that loop from one generation to the next. Children who live in homes where parents smoke are more likely to become smokers. Parents who abuse drugs or alcohol are more likely to find their children someday do the same. Adults who were abused as children may indeed hurt their own children. And that's not all. Parents with a low self-esteem raise children with the same affliction. There are cycles to teenage pregnancy, domestic violence, and under-education. Talk shows thrive on the fallout from cyclical dysfunction.

Just because we know cycles exist doesn't mean researchers have determined exactly what causes them. Current thought is that some of children's behaviors are related to biological factors and some to environmental factors. (Sounds logical to me.) For instance, scientists hypothesize that some children inherit a gene that pre-disposes them to low impulse control.

Environmental factors, such as nurturing during early brain development or early exposure to violence, then affect how a child manages impulse control. The theory [implies] that children raised amidst domestic violence, will more likely develop into hostile and aggressive adults. A child raised in a home that handles disagreements non-violently through respectful negotiation would still struggle with a short temper, but would likely learn problem-solving skills that preclude violence. So, a lot of people, those with folk wisdom and those with professional degrees, believe parents play a major role in how our children turn out. Parents give kids their genes at conception, and then through childrearing, we give them our act to follow, too.

Awareness of cycles is good. But many of us only dwell on the negative implications. Yes, kids are very likely to mimic our self-destructive behaviors. But, if we do a good job of parenting, it means children also get a lot of good things from us! We know parents with good self-esteem tend to raise children with more secure self-esteem. Parents who succeed in education tend to have children who meet and even surpass their parents' accomplishments. And while it is true that children of divorced families are more likely to divorce, it is also true that children of happily married parents tend to find the same happiness in adult relationships. Why is it easier to believe in negative cycles?

Children Will Copy Us

The most important lesson that cycles teach us is that role modeling can be an extremely effective parenting tool. It is powerful that we should use it to our advantage! Being a positive role model requires fore-thought and self control. Today we talk a lot about disciplining our children. We parents need to put an equal emphasis on disciplining ourselves.

It's easy to dispense don'ts to our kids: "Don't smoke." "Don't drink and drive." "Don't do drugs." "Don't lie." It takes

Apologize and Admit Mistakes

Nobody's perfect. When you make a bad choice, let those who are watching and learning from you know that you made a mistake and how you plan to correct it. This will help them to understand that (a) everyone makes mistakes; (b) it's not the end of the world; (c) you can make it right; and (d) you should take responsibility for it as soon as possible. By apologizing, admitting your mistake, and repairing the damage, you will be demonstrating an important yet often overlooked part of being a role model.

Robyn J.A. Silverman, Powerful Parent Blog,
March 31, 2008. www.drrobynsilverman.com

much more effort and discipline to practice what we preach. It takes a strong character to give our kids a good role model to copy, because copy us they will. What a disservice we do to them if we only give them self-destructive behaviors as a road map to follow in life. If you don't want your kids dying of lung cancer, a wise strategy would be to stop smoking yourself. (And if you think you can sneak a cigarette when the kids aren't looking, you are wrong; they smell it.) If we don't want the kids lying to get out of going to school, we best not lie about taking a "sick" day from work.

Challenge yourself to identify the positive things you can role model for your kids—things like happiness, consideration, self-respect, patience, generosity, self-discipline, diligence, kindness, bravery, and compassion. Role model feeding your body with wholesome and nourishing food, expanding your mind with enlightening reading, exercising for physical and mental health, speaking well about yourself and others, and enjoying life with friends and family.

Kids respect adults who walk their talk. Children are sensitive and astute with an uncanny ability to distinguish between adults who only talk a good game and those who play the game by the rules they preach. Credible adults inspire kids' confidence and admiration. Hypocrisy disillusions children and sends them looking for others to follow.

It turns out that folk wisdom is right after all—"Seeing is believing." What kids see and believe, they become. Each and every day, parents build a legacy for kids to inherit. Choose to be a parent who role models family traits worth believing in and worth building upon. After all, what goes around, comes around . . . unceasingly from one generation to the next.

"By [spending ethically] we can have an impact on the larger economy and help create a world where the economy benefits all people in more equal ways."

People Should Spend Ethically to Minimize the Impacts of Consumption

Women & the Economy

Women & the Economy is a project of UN Platform for Action Committee Manitoba in Canada. In the following viewpoint, Women & the Economy urges consumers to use their spending power for the environment and good of communities. For instance, the project states that shopping at homegrown businesses instead of "big-box stores" supports the local economy and cuts down on pollution. Consideration should be given to the environmental and social costs of a product, adds the authors, and consumers should buy organic produce, secondhand items, and fair-trade goods whenever possible.

As you read, consider the following questions:

1. What questions should consumers ask retailers and businesses, in Women & the Economy's opinion?

"Ethical Consumption," UNPAC, September, 2009. Reproduced by permission.

2. According to the authors, how does donated clothing harm developing countries?

3. What is fair trade, as described by Women & the Economy?

Many women have chosen to pay close attention to how they spend their dollars. As [Canadian environmental activist] Robin [Faye] explains, "When I go to spend money I'm making decisions based on where that money's going to go after. Is it going to be used against me or somebody like me someplace else in the world or is it going to actually contribute to building a world where the things that I value are also treasured?" The following suggestions for ethical consumption are not meant to make people feel guilty about buying things or to feel overwhelmed with yet another task. Ethical consumption is a way to help us feel that we have power as consumers, that we can vote with our dollars. By using this consumer power we can have an impact on the larger economy and help create a world where the economy benefits all people in more equal ways. Here are some suggestions for ethical consumption:

1. *Support local businesses.*

   By supporting locally owned businesses we are contributing to our local economy. In contrast, when we buy things at big stores that are owned by people at the other end of the country or the world, our money disappears into a corporation we know little about and which is probably located far from our homes. By keeping our money within our own community we increase the likelihood that it will be used to strengthen our community.

2. *Make a point about asking about the people who made the things you buy.*

Sometimes it's a little tough to ask questions like, "Can you tell me about the working conditions of the people who sewed this shirt?" but it sure gets the attention of retailers and other shoppers! When asked, many of them will admit they have concerns too. Ask to sign a comment card at stores you visit and be sure to ask for follow-up. For example, ask the company to send you a copy of their code of conduct. Also, make a point of telling companies that you'd be willing to pay more for the product if you could be assured that the people were being treated fairly and getting paid a living wage. After all, author Michael Moore has figured out that if the people who make Nike running shoes were to be paid fairly, the shoes would only cost about $3 more!

3. *Consider the environmental costs of producing the product.*

Pesticides and chemicals are used in the production of many of the products that we buy today. Roses and other cut flowers require huge amounts of pesticides to look perfect. Cotton production is also chemical-intensive. When you can, buy organic, both food and clothing. Don't be afraid when you notice blemishes on your fruits and vegetables. It means that less wax and polish were used and hopefully fewer chemicals too.

4. *Think about how you will dispose of the product once you are finished with it.*

Sometimes we buy things that won't last very long or maybe we're not sure if we like them but since they don't cost much we don't think about it. However, buying things that are going to be thrown away soon makes a negative contribution to our environment. In the end it would probably be a better idea for us to buy something that we really want and that we plan to use for years to come. Also, when we buy things made of plastic we can expect that they will be around for thousands of years following our use of them (most plastics are not recycled even if they can be). Many wood and plant products, on the other hand, will eventually break down. Although paper and metal can be recycled, the production of these products contributes negatively to our environment.

5. *Consider buying second-hand.*

Buying second-hand takes a little patience but it can be very entertaining searching through things others have passed on and you'll often find incredible buys. When you are buying second-hand, not only do you get great deals but you also help clean up our society's 'garbage' instead of purchasing more new things that will eventually need to be thrown away. (A lot of extra second-hand clothing in Canada gets shipped to countries in Africa and Asia devastating their local economies and creating a 'need' for western styles.) Many thrift and second-hand stores support community development locally and globally. MCC Thrift Stores support projects in developing countries around the world, Goodwill Stores support local employment projects, and locally-owned independent thrift stores contribute to local community economic development.

6. *Support fair trade.*

Fair trade is a form of trade that guarantees producers a fair price for their product. Fair trade also educates consumers on the importance of paying a fair price for products and works towards environmental sustainability. Fair trade coffee and tea are becoming more and more available. . . . Certain stores, such as Ten Thousand Villages, sell only fair trade products. Next time you are shopping for a gift, consider buying fair trade. Sometimes these products cost a little more but if you include a note explaining where the product is from, who

What Is Ethical?

Ethical practice is about more than just fair-trade, it is more than organic, it involves holistic appraisal of every aspect that goes into the trade and industry behind a product or service; in Marxist terms it is the "means of production and distribution." There is no one definition for "ethical." As an adjective it's very nature is open to interpretation, although there is no doubt that to be ethically led means to be trying to "do the right thing" at all points of the supply chain.

Ethical Pulse, "The Tale of Two Tomatoes,"
July 29, 2009. www.ethical-junction.org.

made it, and that the gift itself is a gift to the person who made it, then it may be alright for you to give something a little smaller than you would otherwise. . . .

7. *Consider the transportation required.*

Think how far the product had to travel to reach you. Was it many thousands of kilometres or just a few? What is the impact of this on the environment? Think too about the distance you had to travel to reach the product. Travelling across town to save a couple of dollars uses time and produces pollution. Walking to the neighbourhood store to buy something that may cost a little more gives us an opportunity to talk to our neighbours contribute to our local economy while exercising our bodies.

8. *Buy local products and services.*

Although no region produces everything its residents desire, there are many ways we can become more dependant on local goods and services. We can support our local economies by buying gift items unique to our region, avoiding big box stores, and support local artists, musicians, and authors by buying their work. Eating local produce means supporting food-producers in our region and reducing the need for food to be transported great distances.

9. *Eat slow food.*

Eating at restaurants, especially fast-food outlets, requires substantially more of the earth's energy than eating at home. When you do eat out, support locally-owned restaurants whose owners contribute to your community rather than large chain restaurants whose owners take their profits far away from your community. Eating vegetarian or vegan will also reduce your consumption. Producing 1 kg of meat requires 10kg of grain so by eating grains and vegetables directly we can soften our impact on the earth. Eating fewer pre-packaged meals reduces waste and can also save money. Although cooking takes time, sharing meals with friends and family at your own home can be a truly nurturing activity.

10. *Reuse things. Fix things that are broken.*

Instead of throwing something away, take the time to fix it yourself. Or bring it to a local tradesperson to fix for you. The cost may be cheaper than buying a new one and you'll also be helping reduce waste.

11. *Don't get sucked in by advertising.*

The job of advertisers is to try to convince people to buy things they usually don't need. Don't get sucked in. In fashion, create your own style. Compliment people who go against the trends. In this way you'll also be creating a more accepting world for people who can't afford all the latest goods.

12. *Buy less stuff and be willing to pay a bit more for what you do buy.*

    Try not to buy things just on a whim, especially if they will take up a lot of room and won't disappear from the earth in the near future. By limiting our purchases we can use the money we save to pay a more appropriate price for what we do buy. When buying something don't just consider the immediate financial cost to yourself. Consider what costs the purchase will have on the producer, the environment, and the community.

13. *Invest your money locally and ethically.*

    When investing your money invest locally. Use your local credit union instead of a large bank. When buying RRSPs [registered retirement savings plans] and other investments ask questions about what your money will be used for. Many so-called 'ethical' investments are not very convincing but more and more organizations are paying good attention to the kind of economic activity they are supporting. . . .

14. *Stay cheerful and committed.*

    Know that everything you do, no matter how small, is making a difference. Instead of being frustrated about what you can't do, recognize what you can do and do it well.

Periodical Bibliography

The following articles have been selected to supplement the diverse views presented in this chapter.

Gary Gardner — "Hungry for More: Re-engaging Religious Teachings on Consumption," *World Watch*, September–October 2005.

Anand Giridharadas — "Expressing Convictions at the Mall," *New York Times*, October 9, 2009.

Global Agenda — "Why Does Berkeley Have So Many Priuses?" June 16, 2008.

Ashley Merryman — "Are Good Deeds a License to Misbehave?" NurtureShock blog (*Newsweek*), October 12, 2009. http://blog.newsweek.com/blogs/nurtureshock/default.aspx.

J. Karl Miller — "Decline of Moral Behavior Painful to Watch," *Columbia Missourian*, March 24, 2009. www.columbiamissourian.com.

Steven Parker — "Who Are Your Children's Role Models?" WebMD, February 12, 2009. www.webmd.com.

Lucy Siegle — "Where Did It All Go Right?" *Guardian* (Manchester, UK), October 29, 2006. www.guardian.co.uk.

Robyn Silverman — "Powerful Role Models: Seven Ways to Make a Positive Impact on Children," Dr. Robyn Silverman, March 31, 2008. www.drrobynsilverman.com.

Glen Stassen — "The Ten Commandments Should Be Interpreted as Deliverance for the Vulnerable," *Tikkun*, March–April 2009.

Jess Worth — "Buy Now, Pay Later," *New Internationalist*, November 2006.

**OPPOSING
VIEWPOINTS®
SERIES**

CHAPTER 2

What Motivates People to Behave Ethically?

Chapter Preface

In late 2009, researchers claimed to have conducted experiments in which people exposed to the "clean" scent of citrus Windex showed more fairness and charity. "There is a strong link between moral and physical purity that people associate at a core level. People feel contaminated by immoral choices and try to wash away their sins," contends Katie Liljenquist, lead author of the study and professor at Brigham Young University's Marriot School of Management. "To some degree, washing actually is effective in alleviating guilt. What we wondered was whether you could regulate ethical behavior through cleanliness. We found that we could."

In the fairness experiment, subjects were given $12 by an unknown partner (who expected them to split it evenly) and were left to decide how much to return and keep for themselves. People in a room with no smell gave back an average of $2.81; those in a room sprayed with Windex averaged $5.33. In the charity experiment, subjects were surveyed on their interests in volunteering for Habitat for Humanity with a school organization and giving money to the cause. On a scale from 1 to 7, subjects in a room with no smell showed an interest of 3.29. People in the room with the Windex scent demonstrated an interest of 4.21. Furthermore, only 6 percent subjected to no smell wanted to donate money, contrasting with 22 percent exposed to the smell of Windex. "Researchers have known for years that scents play an active role in reviving positive or negative experiences," claims Adam Galinsky, a coauthor of the study from the Kellogg School of Management at Northwestern University. "Now, our research can offer more insight into the links between people's charitable actions and their surroundings." In the following chapter, the authors attempt to identify the motivations for ethical behavior.

> *"In the Judeo-Christian value system, God is the source of moral values and therefore what is moral and immoral transcends personal or societal opinion."*

Judeo-Christian Values Motivate People to Behave Ethically

Dennis Prager

Based in Los Angeles, California, Dennis Prager is a host of a nationally syndicated radio talk show and author of several books, including Happiness Is a Serious Problem. *In the following viewpoint, Prager declares that Judeo-Christian values are inseparable from ethics and morality. He posits that reason and rationality can justify unethical as well as ethical acts, and without God as a source of right and wrong, moral relativism has become the prevailing attitude in society. Furthermore, the secular value system has demeaned human worth to that equal to animals, Prager concludes.*

Dennis Prager, "Better Answers: The Case for Judeo-Christian Values, Parts III, IV and Moral Absolutes: The Case for Judeo-Christian Values, Part XI," FrontPageMag.com, January–May, 2005. Reproduced by permission of Creators Syndicate, Inc.

As you read, consider the following questions:

1. In Prager's view, why is reason alone incapable of leading to moral conclusions?

2. According to the author, what mistake do followers of Judeo-Christian values make about moral relativism?

3. Why does the Judeo-Christian value system elevate human worth, as stated by Prager?

Those who do not believe that moral values must come from the Bible or be based upon God's moral instruction argue that they have a better source for values: human reason.

In fact, the era that began the modern Western assault on Judeo-Christian values is known as the Age of Reason. That age ushered in the modern secular era, a time when the men of "the Enlightenment" hoped they would be liberated from the superstitious shackles of religious faith and rely on reason alone. Reason, without God or the Bible, would guide them into an age of unprecedented moral greatness.

As it happened, the era following the decline of religion in Europe led not to unprecedented moral greatness, but to unprecedented cruelty, superstition, mass murder and genocide. But believers in reason without God remain unfazed. Secularists have ignored the vast amount of evidence showing that evil on a grand scale follows the decline of Judeo-Christian religion.

Four Primary Problems

There are four primary problems with reason divorced from God as a guide to morality.

The first is that reason is amoral. Reason is only a tool and, therefore, can just as easily argue for evil as for good. If you want to achieve good, reason is immensely helpful; if you want to do evil, reason is immensely helpful. But reason alone cannot determine which you choose. It is sometimes rational to do what is wrong and sometimes rational to do what is right.

It is sheer nonsense—nonsense believed by the godless— that reason always suggests the good. Mother Teresa devoted her life to feeding and clothing the dying in Calcutta. Was this decision derived entirely from reason? To argue that it was derived from reason alone is to argue that every person whose actions are guided by reason will engage in similar self-sacrifice, and that anyone who doesn't live a Mother Teresa-like life is acting irrationally.

Did those non-Jews in Europe who risked their lives to save a Jew during the Holocaust act on the dictates of reason? In a lifetime of studying those rescuers' motives, I have never come across a single instance of an individual who saved Jews because of reason. In fact, it was irrational for any non-Jews to risk their lives to save Jews.

Another example of reason's incapacity to lead to moral conclusions: On virtually any vexing moral question, there is no such thing as a purely rational viewpoint. What is the purely rational view on the morality of abortion? Of public nudity? Of the value of an animal versus that of a human? Of the war in Iraq? Of capital punishment for murder? On any of these issues, reason alone can argue effectively for almost any position. Therefore, what determines anyone's moral views are, among other things, his values—and values are beyond reason alone (though one should be able to rationally explain and defend those values). If you value the human fetus, most abortions are immoral; if you only value the woman's view of the value of the fetus, all abortions are moral.

The second problem with reason alone as a moral guide is that we are incapable of morally functioning on the basis of reason alone. Our passions, psychology, values, beliefs, emotions and experiences all influence the ways in which even the most rational person determines what is moral and whether to act on it.

Third, the belief in reason alone is itself based on an irrational belief—that people are basically good. You have to believe that people are basically good in order to believe that human reason will necessarily lead to moral conclusions.

Fourth, even when reason does lead to a moral conclusion, it in no way compels acting on that conclusion. Let's return to the example of the non-Jew in Nazi-occupied Europe. Imagine that a Jewish family knocks on his door, asking to be hidden. Imagine further that on rational grounds alone (though I cannot think of any), the non-Jew decides that the moral thing to do is hide the Jews. Will he act on this decision at the risk of his life? Not if reason alone guides him. People don't risk their lives for strangers on the basis of reason. They do so on the basis of faith—faith in something that far transcends reason alone.

Does all this mean that reason is useless? God forbid. Reason and rational thought are among the hallmarks of humanity's potential greatness. But alone, reason is largely worthless in the greatest quest of all—making human beings kinder and more decent. To accomplish that, God, a divinely revealed manual and reason are all necessary. And even then there are no guarantees.

But if you want a quick evaluation of where godless reason leads, look at the irrationality and moral confusion that permeate the embodiment of reason without God—your local university. . . .

Moral Relativism

Nothing more separates Judeo-Christian values from secular values than the question of whether morality—what is good or evil—is absolute or relative. In other words, is there an objective right or wrong, or is right or wrong a matter of personal opinion?

In the Judeo-Christian value system, God is the source of moral values and therefore what is moral and immoral transcends personal or societal opinion. Without God, each society or individual makes up its or his/her moral standards. But once individuals or societies become the source of right and wrong, right and wrong, good and evil, are merely adjectives describing one's preferences. This is known as moral relativism, and it is the dominant attitude toward morality in modern secular society.

Moral relativism means that murder, for example, is not objectively wrong; you may feel it's wrong, but it is no more objectively wrong than your feeling that some music is awful renders that music objectively awful. It's all a matter of personal feeling. That is why in secular society people are far more prone to regard moral judgments as merely feelings. Children are increasingly raised to ask the question, "How do you feel about it?" rather than, "Is it right or wrong?"

Only if God, the transcendent source of morality, says murder is wrong, is it wrong, and not merely one man's or one society's opinion.

Most secular individuals do not confront these consequences of moral relativism. It is too painful for most decent secular people to realize that their moral relativism, their godless morality, means that murder is not really wrong, that "I think murder is wrong," is as meaningless as "I think purple is ugly."

That is why our culture has so venerated the Ten Commandments—it is a fixed set of God-given moral laws and principles. But that is also why opponents of America remaining a Judeo-Christian country, people who advocate moral relativism, want the Ten Commandments removed from all public buildings. The Ten Commandments represents objective, i.e., God-based, morality.

All this should be quite clear, but there is one aspect of moral relativism that confuses many believers in Judeo-Christian moral absolutes. They assume that situational ethics is the same thing as moral relativism and therefore regard

The Infinite Source

An absolute standard of morality can only stem from an infinite source. Why is that?

When we describe murder as being immoral, we do not mean it is wrong just for now, with the possibility of it becoming "right" some time in the future. Absolute means unchangeable, not unchanging.

What's the difference?

My dislike for olives is unchanging. I'll never start liking them. That doesn't mean it is *impossible* for my taste to change, even though it's highly unlikely. Since it *could* change, it is not absolute. It is changeable.

The term "absolute" means without the *ability* to change. It is utterly permanent, unchangeable.

Nechemia Coopersmith,
"Morality: Who Needs God?"
March 25, 2000. www.aish.com.

situational ethics as incompatible with Judeo-Christian morality. They mistakenly argue that just as allowing individuals to determine what is right and wrong negates moral absolutes, allowing situations to determine what is right and wrong also negates moral absolutes.

This is a misunderstanding of the meaning of moral absolutes. It means that if an act is good or bad, it is good or bad for everyone in the identical situation ("universal morality").

But "everyone" is hardly the same as "every situation." An act that is wrong is wrong for everyone in the same situation, but almost no act is wrong in every situation. Sexual intercourse in marriage is sacred; when violently coerced, it is rape. Truth telling is usually right, but if, during World War II, Nazis asked you where a Jewish family was hiding, telling them the truth would have been evil.

So, too, it is the situation that determines when killing is wrong. That is why the Ten Commandments says "Do not murder," not "Do not kill." Murder is immoral killing, and it is the situation that determines when killing is immoral and therefore murder. Pacifism, the belief that it is wrong to take a life in every situation, is based on the mistaken belief that absolute morality means "in every situation" rather than "for everyone in the same situation." For this reason, it has no basis in Judeo-Christian values, which holds that there is moral killing (self-defense, defending other innocents, taking the life of a murderer) and immoral killing (intentional murder of an innocent individual, wars of aggression, terrorism, etc.).

But situational ethics aside, the key element to Judeo-Christian morality remains simply this: There is good and there is evil independent of personal or societal opinion; and in order to determine what it is, one must ask, "How would God and my God-based text judge this action?" rather than, "How do I—or my society—feel about it?"

That different religious people will at times come up with different responses in no way negates the fact that at least they may be pursuing moral truth. In secular society, where there is no God-based morality, there is no moral truth to pursue. The consequences may be easily seen by observing that the most morally confused institution in America, the university—where good and evil are often either denied or inverted—is also its most secular. . . .

Human Worth

Would you first save the dog you love or a stranger if both were drowning? The answer depends on your value system.

One of the most obvious and significant differences between secular and Judeo-Christian values concerns human worth. One of the great ironies of secular humanism is that it devalues the worth of human beings. As ironic as it may sound, the God-based Judeo-Christian value system renders man infinitely more valuable and significant than any humanistic value system.

The reason is simple: Only if there is a God who created man is man worth anything beyond the chemicals of which he is composed. Judeo-Christian religions hold that human beings are created in the image of God. If we are not, we are created in the image of carbon dioxide. Which has a higher value is not difficult to determine.

Contemporary secular society has rendered human beings less significant than at any time in Western history.

First, the secular denial that human beings are created in God's image has led to humans increasingly being equated with animals. That is why over the course of 30 years of asking high school seniors if they would first try to save their dog or a stranger, two-thirds have voted against the person. They either don't know what they would do or actually vote for their dog. Many adults now vote similarly.

Why? There are two reasons. One is that with the denial of the authority of higher values such as biblical teachings, people increasingly make moral decisions on the basis of how they feel. And since probably all people feel more for their dog than they do for a stranger, many people without a moral instruction manual simply choose to do what they feel.

The other reason is that secular values provide no basis for elevating human worth over that of an animal. Judeo-Christian values posit that human beings, not animals, are created in God's image and, therefore, human life is infinitely more sacred than animal life.

That is why people estranged from Judeo-Christian values (including some Christians) support programs such as "Holocaust on Your Plate," the People for the Ethical Treatment of Animals (PETA) campaign that teaches that there is no difference between the slaughtering of chickens and the slaughtering of the Jews in the Holocaust. A human and a chicken are of equal worth.

That is why a Tucson, AZ, woman last year screamed to firefighters that her "babies" were in her burning house. Thinking that the woman's children were trapped inside, the firemen risked their lives to save the woman's three cats.

Those inclined to dismiss these examples as either theoretical (the dog-stranger question) or extreme (the Tucson mother of cats) need to confront the very real question of animal experimentation to save human lives. More and more people believe as PETA does that even if we could find a cure for cancer or AIDS, it would be wrong to experiment on animals. (The defense that research with computers can teach all that experiments on animals teach is a lie.) In fact, many animal rights advocates oppose killing a pig to obtain a heart valve to save a human life.

Belief in human-animal equivalence inevitably follows the death of Judeo-Christian values, and it serves not so much to elevate animal worth as to reduce human worth. Those who oppose vivisection and believe it is immoral to kill animals for any reason, including eating, should reflect on this: While there are strong links between cruelty to animals and cruelty to humans, there are no links between kindness to animals and kindness to humans. Kindness to animals has no effect on a person's treatment of people. The Nazis, the cruelest group in modern history, were also the most pro-animal rights group prior to the contemporary period. They outlawed experimentation on animals and made legal experimentation on human beings.

The second reason that the breakdown of Judeo-Christian values leads to a diminution of human worth is that if man was not created by God, the human being is mere stellar dust—and will come to be regarded as such. Moreover, people are merely the products of random chance, no more designed than a sand grain formed by water erosion. That is what the creationism-evolution battle is ultimately about—human worth. One does not have to agree with creationists or deny all evolutionary evidence to understand that the way evolution is taught, man is rendered a pointless product of random forces—unworthy of being saved before one's hamster.

> "One cannot act ethically if motivated by a command or a commandment, and motivation matters, not just in the abstract, but in the real world of rewards and punishments."

Judeo-Christian Values Do Not Motivate People to Behave Ethically

David Koepsell

In the following viewpoint, David Koepsell asserts that religious morality is unethical. Responding to the criticism that atheists do not have moral absolutes, he accuses Jews and Christians of being moral relativists themselves; they subjectively pick and choose commandments, ignoring many that are outright immoral or nonsensical. The claim that God's authority may not be questioned is also problematic, Koepsell says, because interpretations of commandments vary from and contradict each other. Ultimately, the author maintains that ethical behavior must be more than a list of good and bad behaviors prescribed by religion. Koepsell is executive director of the Council for Secular Humanism.

David Koepsell, "The Immorality of Religious Ethics," *Secular Humanist Bulletin*, vol. 23, Fall 2007, copyright © 2007 by the Council for Secular Humanism. All rights reserved. Reproduced by permission.

As you read, consider the following questions:

1. What are some commandments Koepsell claims are ignored by Christians and Jews?

2. What is the goal of normative ethics, in the author's view?

3. How does Koepsell support his claim that ethical behavior is rooted in biology and evolution?

One of the frequent and abhorrent objections made to or about nonbelievers is that we have no foundation for ethics, no moral compass, as it were. Without a god to guide us in our everyday communion with our fellow humans, we must be drifting in a sea of relativism, guided by animal instincts, hedonistic desires, and acting moment to moment to fulfill our individual interests. As expressed on the Web site ChristianAnswers.[net]: "Atheism leads most Secular Humanists to adopt ethical Relativism—the belief that no absolute moral code exists, and therefore man must adjust his ethical standards in each situation according to his own judgment. If God does not exist, then He cannot establish an absolute moral code. Humanist Max Hocutt says that human beings 'may, and do, make up their own rules. . . . Morality is not discovered; it is made.'"

In my experience, this just isn't so. This myth is based upon a number of conceits that do not stand up against the weight of the evidence. Chief among these is the notion that morals come from some higher power and that humankind, were it not for the beneficent and stern guidance of its supernatural dictator, would devolve into a Hobbesian [according to the English philosopher Thomas Hobbes] war of all against all. This thesis is objectionable for a number of reasons, and it ultimately devalues human morality as found in nature and as expressed in everyday acts of beneficence and kindness. Ultimately, those of us who come to our ethics via secular means often marvel at the grand hypocrisy of religious proselytizers who chide their congregations into accepting millennia-old ethical codes handed down from primitive, hierarchical societies, picking and choosing those commandments they believe worthy and conveniently forgetting those that make no sense in our modern world. Isn't this a form of ethical relativism?

Picking and Choosing

It is easy to find examples. Modern Jews and Christians ignore wholesale a range of clearly crazy commandments from their holy texts. Take, for instance, some famous examples of laws handed down by the Judaic God, which though they might not have fit onto Moses' tablets, nonetheless had the force of law:

- Don't let cattle graze with other kinds of Cattle. (Leviticus 19:19)

- Don't have a variety of crops on the same field. (Leviticus 19:19)

- Don't wear clothes made of more than one fabric. (Leviticus 19:19)

- Don't cut your hair nor shave. (Leviticus 19:27)

- Any person who curseth his mother or father, must be killed. (Leviticus 20:9)

- Anyone who dreams or prophesizes anything that is against God, or anyone who tries to turn you from God, is to be put to death. (Deuteronomy 13:5)

- If anyone, even someone from your own family, suggests worshiping another god, kill them. (Deuteronomy 13:6–10)

- If you find out a city worships a different god, destroy the city and kill all of its inhabitants . . . even the animals. (Deuteronomy 13:12–15)

- Kill anyone with a different religion. (Deuteronomy 17:2–7)

So clearly (and thankfully) almost every Christian and Jew picks and chooses which commandments to follow and which ones to disobey. Let's hope Pope Benedict [XVI, elected to the papacy in 2005] doesn't turn back the clock so far as to require obedience to the letter of the law—although it seems he's working on it, having recently declared Catholicism the One True Church. (If he decided this meant killing all non-Catholics, at least the Scriptures would back him up.) This kind of thinking is, of course, a form of relativism, and it undermines attacks made by believers on those of us who choose to look for ethics through reason, rather than dogma.

Obviously, the dogma and specific commands of each religion can be critically examined, picked apart, and questioned for their current relevance, common sense, or usefulness in general. A more interesting question, and one that most of us are wont to ask, is "By what authority is a commandment valid?" The self-sealing argument of believers is that the authority is God's. Numerous problems arise then, not only as believers pick and choose which commandments to follow but as multiple drafts of commandments emerge and conflict with one another. The commandment, for instance, to not kill is contradicted by other commandments. Modern interpretations of ancient strictures, moreover, complicate matters even further. Consider the case of adultery, which is specifically prohibited by the famous Ten Commandments but is a narrower crime in the Bible than under, for instance, Alabama law. The biblical definition of adultery is the breach of a marriage contract and occurs when a man (married or unmarried) has sexual intercourse with a woman who is either married or betrothed to another man. ([President] Bill Clinton was clearly reading his Bible carefully. [The woman with whom the married Clinton had a sexual relationship was not married or engaged.]) By biblical definition, my ancient namesake, King

A Wholly Human Construct

Morality is a wholly human construct; valid arguments can be made that humanists, by virtue of their lack of a bible or other simplistic guidebook, spend a greater amount of time evaluating the ethics of their decisions, and may be, in many respects, more consciously moral than their religious brethren. Humanists must establish their moral status on a par with those practicing traditional religions, and have their opinions and concerns given equal consideration in matters of morality, ethics, and social progress.

Steven F. Goldberg,
Human Perspectives II: The WASH, *2007.*

David, committed adultery with Bathsheba, while Clinton was only a fornicator. David the adulterer wasn't impeached; nor was he put to death. It's good to be king.

The God of the commandments demands subservience and tolerates no questioning, no appeals. His authority may not be questioned either, and his commandments are, for all time, etched in stone—except when they are conveniently forgotten or reframed by new uses of language. These ancient rules seem quaint now, and we can understand the temptation of most Christians to chuck those bits that make no sense and keep those that seem to accord with universal values (like not murdering people). But is this ethics, and can one who says that he or she abides by the commands of an unquestionable authority, but picks and chooses among them, be said to be acting morally? We can do so under some conceptions of ethics, perhaps, but not if we are serious about the existence of the good.

Moral Intuitions

One of the great remaining problems in philosophy concerns describing the nature of morals and reconciling numerous disparate schools of philosophical ethics. Empiricism has brought remarkable success to studies of the natural world. The sciences have given us ever greater understanding of our universe and the ability to make predictions about it and exert influence over it. We have a nearly complete model of the subatomic realm and can now peer into the deepest reaches of space, back to the expansion of our universe. We can model with great precision the biological processes responsible for life, and we are coming to understand the role of that remarkable strand that ties all earthly life together—DNA. Yet philosophers remain at odds as to ethics, which says more about philosophers than morality. Still, for those of us who concern ourselves with ethics and the nature of morals, this is an exciting time.

The challenge of any ethical system is to accurately describe the nature of the good and to give sound reasons for people to choose the good over the not so good. Alternatives to this challenge include rejecting the distinction between the good and the bad and denying that these distinctions are meaningful beyond a particular subset of people or over a significant span of time. These alternatives are, in fact, part and parcel of the slander leveled against the nonreligious for ages. If you don't believe in a god, it is said, you can choose to do any old thing. You could murder your children, a crime most of us would agree is reprehensible even when ordered by a god and even when your name is Abraham. So, the theist argues that, because his or her god has listed a spate of crimes, she can know with certainty that certain things are wrong, certain things are permissible, and still others, commendable. This list is provisional no less than that of the accused immoral nontheist, as the theist's list is amendable at any time by the drafter: God. Today, killing is allowed, although thou shalt not usually kill. The victims aren't of your tribe, so they don't really count.

Consider, for a moment, the possibility that there is no right or wrong, that all our choices are contingent, equally permissible, and of equal moral worth. The nihilistic alternative could be the case, but it ceases to be an ethical system and leads us to wonder from whence spring our "moral intuitions." Most of us happen to agree on the morality or at least the desirability of certain outcomes over others. Innocents ought not to be slain in their sleep. Automobiles ought not to be stolen. Wars should not be fought based on lies. These intuitions are so prevalent, even among the godless, that most of us are led to the conclusion that they exist for good reason. Philosophers may disagree as to the source of the good, but most rational people distinguish good from bad in remarkably similar ways. [Philosopher and secular humanist] Paul Kurtz has spent much of his lifetime describing the common moral decencies, shared by most ethical systems and cultures around the world and that serve as the basis of ethical decision-making for most of us. We have come a long way, in many respects, from the notion of dogma as a sufficient source of ethical knowledge, but we still seem to have a long way to go.

Any ethical code requires more than a list of good and bad behaviors. Good empiricists, faced with proscriptions or commands regarding a set of behaviors or a collection of ends, must ask: why? This is the unfinished task of ethics. All sciences seek to uncover the causes, reasons, and connections between inputs and outputs. If ethics fails to do this, it will fail as a scientific pursuit. It is still relevant, if we are to delve into ethics as a field of study worthy of scientific rigor, to ask for reasons. What requires us to do such and such or to avoid doing so and so? Why must we develop this or that virtue? And failing to abide by these duties, obligations, virtues, or proscriptions, what warrants our judgment? Normative ethics attempts to develop a set of rules governing human conduct or a set of norms for action. It deals with what people *should* believe to be right and wrong, as distinct from descriptive ethics, which deals with what people *do* believe to be right and wrong. Hence, normative ethics is sometimes said to be prescriptive rather than descriptive. We are concerned with normative ethics, and the major contending schools of normative ethics are virtue ethics, utilitarianism, and deontological [duty-based] ethics. All three of these are in a stalemate, intellectually speaking. Is there a resolution? Is there some reconciliation? Can ethics proceed from this stalemate?

Biological Roots

We secular humanists believe it can. While the current state of philosophical ethics is troubling, other promising developments are under way or on the horizon. In fact, the common moral decencies, shared across borders and throughout time, seem to be rooted in something very real. Recent studies in evolutionary psychology and neurology are revealing biological roots to behaviors we consider ethical. Being good makes good evolutionary sense. Cooperation conveys evolutionary advantages. Studies of a range of animal groups reveal behaviors similar to those we humans believed ourselves privileged to carry out. God doesn't so much command us to be good as do those selfish genes that use us as the shell for their travels throughout time. We aren't all that special. Ironic, then, that the two things that do seem to make us somewhat special—our capacity for cognition and our ability (if not necessarily our propensity) to reason—are what seems most to complicate the process of being ethical. Even more ironic, the one sure way of being unethical, of failing utterly to live up to any moral ideal, is to follow a commandment rather than act according to a principle.

"Religious ethics" is an oxymoron, like "military intelligence" or "jumbo shrimp." One cannot act ethically if motivated by a command or a commandment, and motivation matters, not just in the abstract, but in the real world of rewards and punishments. We know we can be moral, and we dispel with our own experiences the false public notion that the secular cannot be ethical. But we must still make that case, and explain why.

> *"Millions of years of natural selection have molded a universal moral grammar within our brains that enables us to make rapid decisions about ethical dilemmas."*

Innate Morality Motivates People to Behave Ethically

Marc Hauser, interviewed by Josie Glausiusz

In the following viewpoint, Marc Hauser contends that humans possess an innate moral faculty that allows them to make rapid ethical decisions. He draws an analogy between morality and language—instinctive rules underlie a universal moral grammar. Hauser states, however, that unconscious processes guide ethical judgments and are not accessible to the conscious mind. Furthermore, just as languages vary, seemingly inexplicable differences in moral systems can be seen across cultures, he says. Hauser is an evolutionary biologist and cognitive neurologist at Harvard University. Josie Glausiusz is a science journalist.

As you read, consider the following questions:

1. What does an adaptive morality allow, in Hauser's opinion?

Josie Glausiusz, "Is Morality Innate and Universal? An Interview with Marc Hauser," *Discover*, v. 28, May 10, 2007. Reproduced by permission of the author.

2. What moral principle is seen in all societies, as stated by Hauser?

3. What is Hauser's view of religion and morality?

A healthy man walks into a hospital where five patients are awaiting organ transplants. Is it morally acceptable to kill the man in order to harvest his organs to save the lives of five others? If you instantly answered no, you share a near-universal response to the dilemma, one offered by peoples and cultures all over the globe. But how did you reach this conclusion? Was it a rational decision learned in childhood, or was it—as Harvard evolutionary biologist and cognitive neuroscientist Marc Hauser claims—based on instincts encoded in our brains by evolution? In his [2006] book *Moral Minds: How Nature Designed Our Universal Sense of Right and Wrong*, Hauser argues that millions of years of natural selection have molded a universal moral grammar within our brains that enables us to make rapid decisions about ethical dilemmas.

To arrive at this radical notion, Hauser draws on his own research in social cooperation, neuroscience, and primate behavior, as well as on the musings of philosophers, cognitive psychologists, and most important, the theories of MIT [Massachusetts Institute of Technology] linguist Noam Chomsky, who in the 1950s proposed that all humans are equipped with a universal linguistic grammar, a set of instinctive rules that underlie all languages. Hauser himself, a professor of psychology, human evolutionary biology, and organismic and evolutionary biology at Harvard and codirector of the school's Mind/Brain/Behavior Initiative, has analyzed the antics of tamarins, vervet monkeys, macaques, and starlings in captivity, as well as rhesus monkeys and chimpanzees in the wild. This research led to his earlier book *Wild Minds: What Animals Really Think* (2001).

Josie Glausiusz: You argue that humans have an innate moral faculty. Can you describe what you mean by this?

Marc Hauser: The basic idea is to ask about the sources of our moral judgments. What are the psychological processes involved when we deliver a moral judgment of right or wrong? The crucial issue to keep in mind here is a distinction between how we judge and what we do. In some cases, our judgments may align very closely with what we would actually do, but on occasions they may be very, very different.

The second point is to draw on an analogy with language and ask whether there might be something like a universal moral grammar, a set of principles that every human is born with. It's a tool kit in some sense for building possible moral systems. In linguistics, there is a lot of variation that we see in the expressed languages throughout the world. The real deep insight of Chomskian [according to American linguist Noam Chomsky] linguistics was to ask the question, "Might this variation at some level be explained by certain common principles of universal grammar?" That allows, of course, for every language to have its own lexicon. The analogy with morality would simply be: There is going to be a suite of universal principles that dictate how we think about the nature of harming and helping others, but each culture has some freedom—not unlimited—to dictate who is harmed and who is helped.

What is the evidence that we draw upon unconscious principles when making moral decisions?

Let's take two examples. A trolley is coming down a track, and it's going to run over and kill five people if it continues. A person standing next to the track can flip a switch and turn the trolley onto a side track where it will kill one but save the five. Most people think that's morally permissible—to harm one person when five are saved. Another case is when a nurse comes up to a doctor and says, "Doctor, we've got five patients in critical care; each one needs an organ to survive. We do not have time to send out for organs, but a healthy person just walked into the hospital—we can take his organs and save the five. Is that OK?" No one says yes to that one. Now, in both cases your action can save five while harming one, so they're identical in that sense. So why the flip-flop? People of different ages, people of different religious backgrounds, people even with different educations typically cannot explain why they think those cases differ. There appears to be some kind of unconscious process driving moral judgments without its being accessible to conscious reflection.

A Moral Code

What is the evidence that infants already have a moral code ingrained in their brains?

I don't think we're ready to say. Studies have shown that infants as young as 15 months are sensitive to the beliefs of others—true versus false beliefs. That's crucial to the moral domain.

There's also this from the work of Elliot Turiel [a cognitive scientist at the University of California at Berkeley]. He said, Look, there's a very important distinction between a social convention and a moral rule. Children by at least the age of 3 or 4 understand that distinction. Here is a simple way of putting it. If a teacher comes into a classroom and says, "Today, class, instead of raising your hand when you want to ask a question, just ask your question. Don't raise your hand." If you ask kids, "Is that OK?" kids will say, "OK, fine." If you tell them, "In our class, we raise our hands to ask questions, but in France they never raise their hands. Is that OK?" "OK." So it's basically open to authority; it's culturally variable.

So that's a social dimension. But now imagine the following situation. The teacher comes into the class and says, "If you're annoyed by a child sitting next to you, just punch him!" You're going to have moral outrage. You can't say that! If you say, "But in France they do," they'd say, "Well, the French are weird; the French can't say that." So it's completely not open to authoritarian override, in a sense, and it's not culturally variable. So you get this kind of fundamental distinction that's coming on fairly early. But first the question is: How does the kid know that it's in the moral zone as opposed to merely the social zone? We don't know.

Why would natural selection have favored the evolution of an innate moral code within our brains?

One possibility is that these principles that I'm describing were not selected for morality. They were favored for other aspects of social cognition and are simply borrowed by morality. What does morality do at a very general level? It sets up, either unconsciously or consciously, rules for navigating the social world. Now, why might it be unconscious? It might be unconscious for exactly the same reason that language is unconscious at some level.

Imagine that every time you would try to talk to me, you had to think about adjectives, nouns, verbs, and where they go. Well, you would never say anything. This conversation would take 10 years to complete. Whereas if it's unconscious, well, you're just jamming through all this information, because the structure of this stuff is just natural to you. My guess is that there is some aspect of morality which is very much like that. If every time you were confronted with a moral issue you actually had to work it through, you would do nothing else. So there's something highly adaptive to the unconscious aspects of not having to think about these things all the time.

Of course, one of the things that makes morality adaptive is that it does allow for a certain level of within-group stability and, therefore, allows for individual fitness to be enhanced from a genetic perspective. So if I live in a world of defectors, I have no chance, whereas if I can find the cooperators and cooperate with them, my own individual fitness will be greatly enhanced. So I want to know who are the individuals I can trust and those I can't trust. At that level, there's been, of course, greater selection for any kind of social group to have certain kinds of principles that allow for group-level stability.

You draw an analogy between Noam Chomsky's theory of a universal grammar and your own concept of a universal moral code. But moral rules, as described in your book, differ across cultures. For example, some societies permit intentional murder, such as honor killings of women who have transgressed that society's sexual codes. How do you explain this?

Let's focus on honor killings. In this country, in its early stage of colonization, the South of the United States was colonized in part by Celtic herders, Irish, and Scotsmen, whereas the North/Northeast was colonized heavily by German potato plow farmers. That kind of colonization set up very different cultural psychologies. The South developed this very macho policy toward the world—if somebody took your cattle, you were going to kill them. That was crucial to your livelihood. Whereas nobody is going to steal a crop of potatoes. If somebody takes a few, who cares? What that machismo led to were these cases where if a man's wife was caught with somebody else, it was not merely permissible for the man to kill his spouse, it was obligatory. Now, let's take the Middle East. They, too, have honor killings in cases of infidelity. But who does the killing is completely different. There it's not the husband. It's the wife's family who is responsible for killing her. There are rules for permissible killing. Who does the killing is simply a parameter in that space of permissibility.

You mention honor killings in cases of infidelity, but sometimes the victim may simply have been caught in public talking to a man who is not her husband. As a Western woman raised in the liberal tradition, I think that is immoral. Yet in societies where honor killings are acceptable, the decision to kill the woman is deemed morally correct. Why?

Let's go back to language. You're a speaker of English. In French, the world "table" is feminine. Why? Isn't that weird? Isn't that incomprehensible? For an English speaker, that's the most bizarre thing in the world! It's incredibly hard to learn. Yet are the French weird? They're not weird. They speak another language.

The analogy to language is to me very profound and important. When you say, "Look, it's weird that a culture would actually kill someone for infidelity," it's no different than us making a language that's got these really weird quirks. Now, here's where the difference is crucial. As English speakers, we can't tell the French: "You idiots. Saying that a word has gender is stupid, and you guys just change the system." But as we have seen historically, one culture telling another culture, "Hey, this is not OK. We do not think it is morally permissible to do clitoridectomies, and you should just stop, and we're going to find international ways to put the constraints on you"—now, that's whoppingly different. But it also captures something crucial. The descriptive level and the prescriptive level are crucially different. How biology basically guides what people are doing is one thing. What we think should happen is really different. That just doesn't arise as a distinction within language.

Unconscious, Inaccessible Principles

Isn't there a big difference between nuances in language and the varying ways in which different societies define murder? A definition of murder seems much more fundamental to human behavior than whether the French language applies gender to nouns and English does not.

That's a great question. I think the way to unpack it is in the following sense. Look, everyone speaks a language. Everyone has a moral system. You can also say, "Look, every language has certain abstract variables, like nouns and verbs." That's true. Now, what I would say is that every culture has got a distinction about intended harms, about actions versus omissions. There are abstractions about the nature of action which play a role in the same kind of way as nouns and verbs do.

My guess is this: It's a hypothesis. There's a huge amount of other work to be done. In the end, I will bet that the anal-

Circumstantial Evidence

Though no one has identified genes for morality, there is circumstantial evidence they exist. The character traits called "conscientiousness" and "agreeableness" are far more correlated in identical twins separated at birth (who share their genes but not their environment) than in adoptive siblings raised together (who share their environment but not their genes). People given diagnoses of "antisocial personality disorder" or "psychopathy" show signs of morality blindness from the time they are children. They bully younger children, torture animals, habitually lie and seem incapable of empathy or remorse, often despite normal family backgrounds. Some of these children grow up into the monsters who bilk elderly people out of their savings, rape a succession of women or shoot convenience-store clerks lying on the floor during a robbery.

Steven Pinker, New York Times, *January 13, 2008.*

ogy will only go so deep. Morality could not be just like language. It's a different system. But my guess is that there will be unconscious, inaccessible principles that will be in some sense like morality. They will not be part of a child's education, and there will be a richness to the child's representations of the world in the moral area that will be as rich as they are in language.

Are there moral principles that hold true across all societies?

People want to say things like "do unto others [as you would have them do unto you]." You see it everywhere. So there's some notion of reciprocity, and that includes both the good and bad. If I have been harmed, there is some notion of revenge which certainly seems to be part of the human psychology. Some level of, "If somebody does something nice for me, I should do something nice back to them" also seems part of the psychology. It may be evolutionarily ancient. Work that we've done on animals suggests some kind of reciprocity, some ancient level of cooperation. So is there a generic rule that says "don't kill others"? No, there's not, because that rule is always adjoined to a caveat, which says, "Well, we kill some people, but not everybody." It's always an in-group, out-group distinction.

What impact does religion have on moral behavior?

I think that for many who come from a religious background, religion is synonymous with morality. Some people think that if you're an atheist, you simply have no morals. That is just wrong. There are an awful lot of people who are atheists who do very, very wonderful things. As an objective question, do people who have religious backgrounds show different patterns of moral judgments than people who are atheists? So far, the answer is a resounding no.

Do you mean that people give the same answers to objective tests of moral reasoning regardless of religious background?

One hundred percent. So far, exactly the same. Here's an example that comes from MIT philosopher Judy Thomson. She was interested in a question of whether the fetus has an obligatory right to the mother's body. So she gives an incredibly apocryphal, crazy example: A woman is lying in bed one morning, and she wakes up to find a man lying in bed unconscious next to her. Another gentleman walks up to her and says: "I'm terribly sorry, but this man right next to you is a world-famous violinist, and he's unconscious and in terrible health. He's in kidney failure, and I hope you don't mind, but we've plugged him into your kidney. And if he stays plugged in for the next nine months, you will save him."

You ask people, "Is that morally permissible?" They're like: "No, it's insane. Of course not." Well, that makes [Thomson's] point exquisitely. It would be nice if she said, "Sure, I love this guy's playing; plug him in." But she's not obligated to do so. Now let me make it like the abortion case. She says, "Yes, I love this guy's violin playing!" Two months into it, she goes: "You know what? This really is a drag," and she unplugs. Now people all of a sudden have a sense that's less permissible than the first case. But here, people who are pro-choice or pro-life do not differ. So the point is, if you take people away from the familiar and you capture some of the critical underlying psychological issues that play into the real-world cases, then you find that the religious effects are minimal.

Do other species have any form of moral faculty?

Certainly sympathy, caretaking, cooperation; those things are there in some animals. The crucial questions are, "Do animals have any sense of what they ought to do?" and "To what extent will animals judge transgressions of others as being wrong in some way?" How we'd ever understand that, I don't know.

> *"A good moral education allows students to balance all relevant factors and come to a reasonable and defensible decision that incorporates self-knowledge and political awareness."*

Schools Can Teach Children to Behave Ethically

Jack Russell Weinstein

Jack Russell Weinstein is an associate professor of philosophy at the University of North Dakota. In the following viewpoint, Weinstein supports moral education in the classroom; however, he suggests that the debate is fundamentally misguided: Contemporary discussions of moral education call for indoctrinating students with Christian values or teaching them to follow—not interpret—a set of specific rules. Instead, he argues, students should be educated to make their own judgments; define their own values; and grasp their individual abilities, limitations, and ethical obligations.

As you read, consider the following questions:

1. What is problematic about teaching Christian values in school, in the author's opinion?

Jack Russell Weinstein, "What Is Moral Education?" Dr. Jack Russell Weinstein's Philosophy Page! June 2006. Originally published in *The Undercurrent*, June 2006. Reproduced by permission of the author.

2. In what case is adopting roles necessary for children, as stated by Weinstein?

3. What is the author's view of abstinence education?

Our children need ethical skills as much as they need any others, and if we wish our children to grow up to be good people and good citizens, we must allow for our institutions of education to help them along their way. The recent focus on school-based moral education is justified. However, contemporary debate about moral education is dishonest in two fundamental ways.

The first is that the dominant model is essentially a conversion tool for Christianity. Abstinence education, prayer in school, and the call for teaching creationism in the place of real biology are all ideological benchmarks. They pressure students to subscribe or act as if they subscribe to a moral code in exchange for a good grade, thereby demanding that non-Christians accept—without any reflection or opportunity to defend their beliefs—that their own moral systems are inferior to those endorsed by the curriculum. Even if students do not actually convert to Christianity, when they act, choose, and believe as if they do, those who want to impose their religious views on others are mollified. Why pluralism is important is a different, albeit related, conversation that I won't address here. Suffice it to say, those people who revert to calling the United States a Christian country in defense of engineering a homogeneous society understand neither justice nor history.

The second way in which the contemporary debate is dishonest is that it lies about how morality works. Its proponents like to pretend that moral behavior comes from following discrete rules, and as a result they teach our children platitudes. In doing so, they reduce complex human behavior to after-the-fact constructs that describe ideal actions independent of context. They also ignore the fact that character is the consequence of numerous factors, including desire, rationality, habit, and accident. Ethical principles are similar to scientific laws: they describe how things operate in a well-functioning system, and they overlap. All ethical prescriptions are interrelated.

Regurgitation Instead of Judgment

Any model of moral education that prescribes teaching specific moral rules is problematic, and not just because the rules are bound to be controversial. As a learning tool, teaching specific moral rules fails because this type of curriculum confuses knowledge and wisdom, and substitutes regurgitation for judgment. It presumes, for example, that if we can repeat the Ten Commandments, we will obey them, and if we can recite the Golden Rule, we will treat people by its precepts. It assumes that morality is limited only to the content of particular prescriptions: rules are meant to be followed; they are not meant to be interpreted. Yet, no rule can be followed without interpretation. There is no moral action without moral judgment, and there can be no moral judgment without understanding. For example, it may be the case that children should respect their elders, but what does respect mean? Are there not such instances when a child should ignore this command, particularly when an elder does not reciprocate respect? A child who understands respect as obedience—as many households suggest—combined with an adult who steps over his or her own moral limits is a recipe for sexual abuse.

This is not to suggest that there isn't a time and place for rule following. Sometimes children are too young to decide how to act and simply have to do what they are told. Sometimes adults are too excited, too stubborn, or simply too self-involved to do what is right. And, of course, there are circumstances that are too urgent for debate, when obedience to authority must take precedence over moral choice. But these are not moments of moral education. They are instances of social engineering, and are exceptions to the rule. No pedagogy or curriculum should be built on the assumption that every decision is a moral or political crisis. Every moment of our lives is not a litmus test for our soul.

Wrong-Headed Pedagogy

To illustrate, there are few more graphic examples of wrong-headed pedagogy than abstinence education. Its fundamental assumption is that if a student is exposed to calls for abstinence enough times, he or she will not have sex. However, as has been shown repeatedly, these programs fail. The vast majority of students who take abstinence pledges have sex before marriage (many within a year of the pledge), and abstinence education has proven no more effective than any other sex education program in minimizing promiscuity. Furthermore, students who are taught abstinence are at higher risk for unwanted pregnancy and sexually transmitted diseases, because the student who has taken the pledge is convinced that sex is not about to happen, even when it is imminent. Sexual decision making becomes embedded in denial. In such a circumstance, there is no recourse for the student to revise his or her decision on the basis of new choices. The proposition "I wasn't planning on having sex, but since I am, I ought to do it in a moral and responsible way by using a condom and being clear about my limits" has no place in abstinence education. This brand of education destroys an individual's capacity for rational and moderate decision making.

My own students illustrate another way in which abstinence education has failed. I teach undergraduates in the conservative and predominantly Christian state of North Dakota. In my ethics courses, during units on sexual ethics, I ask why people should get married. The students offer the same answer at first: to have moral sex. I push the question, and eventually someone mentions having children. It is usually five or six answers before someone brings up the concept of love or soul-mates. Yet, to this date, none of my students have ever suggested that marriage is a joint project for making a better life and for developing one's character and capacities. The main purpose for marriage, my students have been told time and time again, is to have moral sex. This is an empty and narrow picture of an adult relationship. Homosexuality is not destroying the "time honored" tradition of marriage, abstinence education is.

We are witnessing how current moral education fails students. Abstinence education and other curricula built on the same model, teach obedience without thought. They ignore that most education up through college ought to be primarily concerned with teaching students how to learn. Moral education must therefore focus on developing students' capacities, not their individual choices. Proper actions change based on age, circumstance, context, and prevailing social and political conditions. A good moral education allows students to balance all relevant factors and come to a reasonable and defensible decision that incorporates self-knowledge and political awareness.

Intellectual and Moral Virtues

[The ancient Greek philosopher] Aristotle tells us that there are two sets of virtues, moral and intellectual. The former refers to our . . . judgment and understanding; it is imparted through teaching. For Aristotle, doing the right thing is not the same as knowing the right thing. We need intellectual virtue to identify moral virtue in ourselves and others, and we cultivate moral virtue to be of good character and act accordingly. Two thousand years later, [Scottish philosopher] David Hume reminded us of this division with his famous observation that "reason is and ought to be the slave to the passions." In other words, we can tell our children what they should do until we are blue in the face, but until they are motivated to act as they ought to, what we tell them is just background information: you can lead a horse to water but you can't make him drink.

Character Education

Since Americans are by international standards both quite religiously observant and quite religiously diverse, it is not surprising that moral and character education controversies often have a religious source. Particularly after a period when moral education was not on the agenda of most public schools, its return is unsettling to some citizens. Many who are hostile to religion see this renewed interest in moral education as bringing religious perspectives back into the school "through the back door." On the other hand, many religious people are suspicious of its return because they perceive it to be an attempt to undermine their family's religious-based training with a state-sponsored secular humanism. As of the beginning of the twenty-first century, however, the renewed attention to this area has been relatively free of controversy.

Contributing to the positive climate is the use of the term *character* rather than *moral*. While *moral* carries religious overtones for many, the word *character* speaks to good habits and the civic virtues, which hold a community together and allow us to live together in harmony.

StateUniversity.com,
"Moral Education."

We therefore have to develop curricula that motivate students to both want to do the right thing and be able to determine what that thing is, particularly in circumstances they neither expected nor experienced before. This involves not only determining the proper act in any circumstance, but also knowing what it means to be a good person, to have good friends, and to contribute to a good society. The virtue of Aristotle's (far from perfect) system is its holism: moral education ought to be concerned with cultivating the excellent human being and the excellent society one person, and one classroom, at a time. We must aim to create circumstances in which both individual and collective decision making are rational, honest, informed, and experimental. Any ethical system that assumes all moral decisions to be instances of an already determined template of right and wrong will be neither defensible nor compelling. Students want a hand in their own life choices. Why shouldn't they? We all do.

In short, we must redirect contemporary debate away from the partisan squabbling over whose moral rules ought to be taught in the classroom, and figure out the best means to educate students to be able to make their own decisions, discover and pledge allegiance to their own moral rules, and reflect on their own capacities, limitations, and moral commitments. The religious right is wrong. Moral education should not tell students how to act. Instead, it should teach them how to figure things out for themselves.

Periodical Bibliography

The following articles have been selected to supplement the diverse views presented in this chapter.

Dennis Behreant   "Faith: The Triumph of Reason," *New American*, December 24, 2007.

David Brooks   "Where the Wild Things Are," *New York Times*, October 19, 2009.

Daniel Burke   "Atheism 3.0 Finds a Little More Room for Religion," *USA Today*, October 19, 2009.

William Lane Craig   "God Is Not Dead Yet," *Christianity Today*, July 3, 2008.

Dinesh D'Souza   "The Surprising Fact of Morality," *National Review Online*, November 4, 2009.

Philip F. Harris   "The Bridge Between Dogma and Atheism," *American Chronicle*, October 28, 2009.

Jacob Jacoby   "Atheists' Bleak Alternative," *Boston Globe*, December 13, 2006.

Doug McManaman   "The Need to Reclaim Catholic Social Teaching," *Catholic Insight*, June 2007.

Frederick Meekins   "The Moral Argument for God," *American Daily*, November 2, 2009.

Jeremy Sherman   "The Benefits of a Closed Mind," *Psychology Today*, May 11, 2009.

CHAPTER 3

Are Modern Biomedical Practices Ethical?

Chapter Preface

Ashley was born profoundly disabled in Seattle, Washington. She is entering her teens, but has the mind of a three-month-old baby and cannot sit up or swallow food on her own. Ashley is also very small for her age—4'5" and 75 pounds—and will not reach adult size. With approval from the Children's Hospital and Regional Medical Center's ethics board, doctors gave her hormone treatments and removed her breast tissue and uterus when she was six years old—to stunt her growth and spare her the discomfort of sexual maturity and possibility of pregnancy if raped. "Ashley's smaller and lighter size makes it more possible to include her in the typical family life and activities that provide her with needed comfort, closeness, security, and love: meal time, car trips, touch, snuggles, etc.," her parents wrote on their blog. "A fundamental and universal misconception about the treatment is that it is intended to convenience the caregiver; rather, the central purpose is to improve Ashley's quality of life." They call it the "Ashley Treatment."

In 2007, the Ashley Treatment gained worldwide attention after coverage in a medical journal. Critics from the health and disabled community were morally outraged. "Keeping Ashley small is a pharmacological solution for a social failure—the fact that American society does not do what it should to help severely disabled children and their families," argued Arthur Kaplan, director of the University of Pennsylvania's Center for Bioethics. Keenan Wellar, cofounder of the Canadian disability-advocacy group LiveWorkPlay, alleged that the procedures violated the girl's rights: "Infants have human rights even though they can't speak for themselves. Why should Ashley have received any less consideration?"

Others came forward to support Ashley's parents' decision. "If keeping her small makes it possible for her to live a comparatively pain-free existence in the comfort of her family home, then she will enjoy the only human right that could conceivably matter to her," stated Arthur Schafer, director of the Centre for Professional and Applied Ethics at the University of Manitoba, Canada. And in an e-mail sent to Ashley's parents, a nurse practitioner wrote, "I think if those people who are appalled by the treatment would come and see the children in institutions, developing sores because they are so hard to turn, listen to the parents talk who had to put their children in an institution because they could not care for them at home, and would see the bedridden children/adults who are raped and then die during childbirth, the argument would cease." In the following chapter, the authors debate some of medicine's most polarizing ethical issues.

"Close to 70 percent of Americans favor stem-cell research even when it requires embryo destruction."

Embryonic Stem Cell Research Is Ethical

Rosemary Tong

In the following viewpoint, Rosemary Tong argues that embryonic stem cell research is ethically defensible. She maintains that earmarking unused frozen embryos for research is the best moral option, as adoption may be against the donors' wishes and surplus embryos will either be discarded or die in storage. In addition, Tong suggests that embryos not implanted in a woman's body represent only the potential for human life, and using them for scientific purposes is equal to the donation of people's tissues, organs, and bodies. The author is Distinguished Professor of Health Care Ethics and director of the Center for Professional and Applied Ethics at the University of North Carolina at Charlotte.

As you read, consider the following questions:

1. What is the author's position on embryonic gonadal stem cell research?

Rosemary Tong, "Stem-cell Research and the Affirmation of Life," *Conscience*, vol. 28, Autumn 2007, pp. 19–23. Copyright © 2007, Catholics for Choice. All rights reserved. Reproduced by permission.

2. How does Tong respond to concerns raised about embryos produced through somatic cell nuclear transfer?

3. How does the author support her claim that support for stem cell research is growing?

Whether or not they are fully informed about its intricacies, almost everyone in the United States seems to have an opinion about stem-cell research. Stem cells are either totipotent or pluripotent cells: They have the amazing ability to develop into many or even all the different types of cells that constitute the human body. Their cell lines are immortal in the sense that they can be cultivated indefinitely to produce a virtually unlimited supply of cells, testifying to the strength, resilience, and determination of life itself. Although progress in stem-cell research has been somewhat slow due to technical hurdles, political debates, and the moral controversies described below, most scientists believe stem cells will ultimately prove useful in treating damaged human cells and tissues (including major organs), testing pharmaceutical products for safety, studying embryo development, and discovering new gene-therapy techniques. Indeed, according to the Stem Cell Research Foundation, stem-cell research promises to create treatments to help millions of Americans: 58 million with heart disease, 4.3 million with arthritis, 10 million with osteoporosis, 8.2 million with cancer, 4 million with Alzheimer's disease, 1 million with juvenile diabetes, and 250,000 with spinal-cord injuries. These are big promises and ones that excite most people, but particularly aging baby boomers looking for a medical fountain of youth—treatments and pharmaceutical products that will permit them to live vibrant, healthy lives well into their 90s and even 100s.

A limited number of stem cells is found in adults' tissues and in umbilical-cord blood. In addition, recent studies indicate that stem cells may be present in amniotic fluid, the amniotic membrane, and the placenta. Scientists remain divided about the usefulness of these cells. Some think the cells are able to differentiate only into a relatively narrow array of cells (for example, blood stem cells producing blood elements but not nervous tissues). Others are much more enthusiastic. They point out that so far, the only successful stem cell–derived treatments have come from adult or umbilical-cord stem cells. Examples include the use of adult stem cells found in bone marrow to help victims of heart attacks and the use of umbilical-cord stem cells to treat rare enzyme malfunctions like Krabbe's leukodystrophy, a devastating condition that destroys neurological capacities. These same scientists are enthused about recent successes in programming adult mice skin cells back to pluripotent form. The hope is that similar methods can be used to reprogram a wide variety of human cells back to pluripotent form, so that the need for totipotent stem cells is gradually eliminated.

Whatever promise adult stem cells, umbilical-cord blood cells, and amniotic fluid stem cells hold, most stem-cell researchers still think that, at present, the best source of stem cells is either in the gonadal tissue of aborted fetuses or in the inner mass of blastocysts—that is, of embryos in the early days after fertilization.

Moral Controversy

It is not surprising that both embryonic gonadal (EG) stem-cell research and embryonic stem-cell (ES) research generate moral controversy. People who believe that human life and, therefore, human personhood begins at the moment of conception will view such research as morally wrong. They will claim that to destroy an embryo, even for a good purpose such as curing Alzheimer's disease, is as wrong as killing an adult so that his or her organs can be distributed to six or seven other adults who might otherwise die. But is the wrong done in both these cases really of the same kind and magnitude? I think not.

Consider the case of EG stem cells first. National Catholic Bioethics education director Tadeusz Pacholczyk, a priest and neuroscientist, calls it morally permissible to use EG cells from miscarriages, also known as spontaneous abortions, provided the parents give informed consent. Pacholczyk adds, however, that it is morally forbidden to use EG cells from elective abortions, whether or not the parents give informed consent. But what about EG cells from therapeutic abortions—abortions that must be performed to save the mother's life? Are not these abortions more like spontaneous abortions than elective abortions in intent? Chances are that a woman who has to undergo a therapeutic abortion does not want to terminate her pregnancy any more than a woman who has a spontaneous miscarriage. Why, then, should it not be morally permissible to use EG cells from the former's aborted fetus?

In any event, subsequent to any of the three aforementioned kinds of abortion, is it morally worse to use the embryo for research purposes, or to discard it? Provided that a woman does not get pregnant with the deliberate intent to abort her fetus for the purpose of research, it would seem morally good to use EG cells from her aborted fetus potentially to save other human lives. Regulations can be put into place prohibiting parents from directing that EG stem cells removed from their aborted fetuses be used to develop treatments for particular persons, as was the case when a woman allegedly had an abortion so that the tissue from her aborted fetus could be used to treat her father for Parkinson's disease.

Thinking that work with ES cells might be less morally controversial than with EG cells, many researchers have sought to secure ES cells in one of two basic ways, each of which has turned out to present its own moral issues.

The first source of ES cells is the process of in vitro fertilization, which combines sperm and egg ex utero [outside of the uterus] with the intention of transferring the conceptus to a woman's womb for reproductive purposes. When a couple produces more embryos than it is prudent to transfer into the woman's womb, clinicians generally advise the couple to freeze surplus embryos for possible future use. If a couple takes the clinicians' advice, they may sign a contract—unenforceable in most states, incidentally—that specifies their wishes for the surplus embryos, should they decide not to use them after all. Their options include keeping the embryos frozen, discarding them, putting them up for adoption, or earmarking them for research.

If the couple opts to keep their surplus embryos frozen, they will add yet more embryos to the 900,000 already frozen in U.S. embryo banks. In effect, their decision will let their surplus embryos die a slow death, for, unlike stem cells, frozen embryos are not immortal. If the couple opts instead to discard the surplus embryos, they will, in effect, be choosing to abort them. In this instance, men as well as women get to make the abortion decision; both are asked to decide whether to procreate. (On the face of it, it would seem that opponents of abortion should be more troubled about these ex utero abortions than about traditional in utero abortions; after all, frozen surplus embryos do not in any way threaten a woman's life or health. There is no need, in their case, to weigh their right to life against a woman's right to life or bodily integrity.) The couple's other two options—putting the surplus embryos up for adoption or earmarking them for research—are potentially more life-affirming. One problem with putting up surplus embryos for adoption, however, is that there are probably not enough infertile couples who want them. Another problem with adoption is that some couples would rather discard surplus embryos than have other couples bring them to term and rear them; they simply do not want to procreate and cannot come to terms with the thought that somewhere out there, their child is being reared by strangers. For couples with this mindset, as well as those who would otherwise discard their surplus embryos or freeze them, earmarking embryos for stem-cell research would seem the best moral option. At least such research has the goal of enhancing and extending human life.

The second way of obtaining ES cells is to create them specifically for research purposes. Researchers have sought in this way to avoid the personal drama of in vitro fertilization and to secure the best embryos to use for research—freezing and thawing embryos may, after all, damage or degrade them in some way. Some researchers have opted to create their own embryos by combining, in vitro, the genetic material of willing sperm and egg donors. Other researchers are working to perfect a process called somatic-cell nuclear transfer (SCNT), a form of therapeutic cloning. But to date they have had success cloning only animal embryos, not human embryos. Reports that a South Korean researcher had successfully cloned multiple human embryos turned out to be false—indeed, a case of blatant scientific fraud. To create a human embryo via SCNT, researchers must, as in the animal research that led to the birth of the famous cloned sheep Dolly, fuse one of a human donor's somatic cells—say, a skin or blood cell—with a donor egg cell which has had its nucleus removed. The stem cells produced would be genetically identical to the donor's somatic cells and could be implanted in the donor without fear of rejection.

A Middle Course?

One question that has been raised about embryos produced via SCNT is whether they are really embryos. After all, they are not the product of egg and sperm uniting; they are the product of a somatic cell and an enucleated egg fusing. Another question about SCNT is whether women should be paid for their eggs and, if so, how much. Unlike sperm donation, egg donation is an arduous and risky process. Potential egg donors who would not be willing to take risks for free might be willing to take the same risks for $3,000 to $7,000, the range of money women who sell their eggs for reproductive purposes typically get. Is there any good moral reason that a woman who sells her eggs for research purposes should not be paid the same amount as a woman who sells her eggs for reproductive purposes?

In 2001, President George W. Bush's attempt to steer a middle course between embryonic stem-cell research advocacy and opposition struck me as reasonable. Bush proclaimed that federal funds could be used for only certain types of stem-cell research—namely, adult stem-cell research, umbilical cord blood stem-cell research, and embryonic stem-cell research on already existing stem-cell colonies, said to be 78 in number at that time. An opponent of abortion, he reasoned that because there was no way to bring back from the dead the embryos that had been destroyed to create existing stem-cell lines, some good—in the form of treatments for devastating disease—might as well come from their evil origin. However, Bush emphasized in nearly the same breath that no federal money would be available to create additional stem-cell lines from unwanted frozen embryos or deliberately to create new embryos for research purposes. Importantly, Bush's ruling forbade only federal funding for research on stem-cell lines derived after August 9, 2001. It did not forbid state or private funding for such research, substantial amounts of which have been provided to researchers for over a decade now.

What started to change my mind about the reasonableness of Bush's ruling was that, as it turned out, only 23 of the 78 stem-cell lines were available for research purposes. Of the original 78 lines, 7 were duplicates, 31 were in overseas laboratories that were unwilling or unable to transfer them to the National Institutes of Health for safekeeping and distribution, 16 died after being thawed, and one was withdrawn because the embryo donors withheld consent. Of the remaining 23 lines, none was entirely safe. They had been grown in mouse culture or feeders, exposing them to possible contamination.

Therefore, federally funded researchers would not have enough stem-cell colonies with which to work. To produce new colonies for cutting-edge research, they would have to seek funding from states, charitable private foundations such as the Juvenile Diabetes Research Foundation and the Howard Hughes Medical Institute, profit-making corporations such as Geron, or foreign nations with little or nothing in the way of restrictions on stem-cell research.

Although the exodus of scientists from the public domain into the private domain may not strike terror in Americans' hearts, it concerns many members of the bioethics community. To give one example, Dr. Joshua M. Hare, who has conducted stem-cell research funded by the Maryland biotechnology company Osiris Therapeutics, recently commented, "In Ecuador, fetal stem cells, obtained in the Ukraine, are being used to treat patients from the U.S. There are cowboys [i.e., maverick scientists] who want to do this, and are going to do it." Research done in the private realm is far less regulated and ethically disciplined than research done in the public realm.

A Growing Moral Consensus

Adding to what became my entire dissatisfaction with Bush's 2001 ruling was the fact that a majority of Americans do not share the president's view of the morality of the situation. Polling data indicate that close to 70 percent of Americans favor stem-cell research even when it requires embryo destruction. A poll conducted in 2005 by the Genetics and Public Policy Center at Johns Hopkins University indicated that 69 percent of Roman Catholics, 74 percent of Protestants, and 50 percent of Evangelicals supported stem-cell research. To be sure, just because a majority of people favors a practice does not guarantee its moral rightness. However, a growing majoritarian moral consensus on a subject that requires weighing several moral goods and bads against each other may indicate a need to reflect on one's own moral views. Perhaps some change is in order.

The Milestones of Personhood

Another response to the moral question relies, not on the genetic origins of the embryo, but on its staged progress from zygote to baby. There are many milestones in that progress. It makes sense, say those who hold this position, to attribute moral personhood to the fetus only as it reaches certain of those milestones. Implantation and, above all, the formation of the primitive streak, at about 14 days, which sets the fertilized ovum on the way to individuality and initiates the nervous system, seems to many a significant marker of human personhood. Moral obligations can be ascribed only when individuation has taken place, for only then can it be said that the developing entity is at the start of being a person. One might even maintain that only when the fetus has a firm enough hold on existence that it can live independently of its mother do moral duties of significance appear. In this view, viability, the time at which organ systems, particularly the lungs, can function, even with artificial support, is the most suitable milestone to attribute moral personhood.

Al Jonsen, ARCS Lecture, October 30, 2003.

No doubt Americans' growing moral consensus in support of stem-cell research partially explains why the U.S. Congress passed the Stem-Cell Research Enhancement Act in 2006, and a very similar bill in 2007. Both of these bills permitted federal funding for stem-cell research on frozen surplus embryos that would otherwise be discarded. Bush vetoed both bills, simply reiterating his 2001 position, in what seemed a stubborn rather than a thoughtful manner. Chances are that if Bush is still in office when Congress produces another stem-cell bill, further enhanced with a provision for SCNT, the president will go ballistic before he pulls out his veto pen. [As of Bush's last day as president in January 2009, no more stem-cell research bills had crossed his desk.]

On the occasion of his veto of the 2006 Stem-Cell Research Enhancement Act, Bush surrounded himself with 24 "snowflakes"—children who had been adopted from in vitro fertilization clinics when they were still embryos. His point seemed to be that no surplus embryo need be discarded, that they can all be adopted. But, as I noted above, adoptions of surplus embryos are likely to be relatively few.

There is another, feminist point to be made about Bush's "snowflakes." No human embryo is going to be born unless it is implanted in a woman's womb. Conception is a necessary but not sufficient condition for the emergence of human personhood. It merits underscoring that stem-cell researchers have tried, through processes such as altered nuclear transfer, to create pseudo-embryos that cannot implant in a woman's womb. Pseudo-embryos, as well as bona fide embryos that no woman is willing to take into her body, are merely potential for human life—a potentiality that will never be actualized in the form of a human "snowflake," but can nevertheless be used for the good of the human community to which they belong. We who happen to have been of woman born should also try to add to the good of our human community. We are called, for example, to serve as research subjects, to donate our tissues and organs if and when we can, and to give our cadavers to medical schools for the purposes of clinical education. If ex utero embryos' life-giving powers should not go to waste, neither should ours.

"The protection of human life comes first. . . . Whether it is acceptable to destroy a living human being for the purpose of science . . . I think that in that sense, the embryo is our equal."

Embryonic Stem Cell Research Is Unethical

Yuval Levin, interviewed by David Masci

In the following viewpoint, Yuval Levin asserts that the ethical concerns surrounding embryonic stem cell research must be balanced with its promises. While not particularly religious, he insists that life begins at conception and that embryos deserve human equality and the right to life. Levin concludes that alternatives to stem cell research should be pursued in order not to force the choice between science and ethics. Yuval Levin is the Hertog Fellow at the Ethics and Public Policy Center in Washington, D.C., and the director of the center's Bioethics and American Democracy Program. David Masci is a senior research fellow at the Pew Forum on Religion and Public Life.

David Masci, "The Case Against Embryonic Stem Cell Research: An Interview with Yuval Levin," Pew Forum on Religion & Public Life, July 17, 2008. Pew Research Center's Forum on Religion & Public Life, http://www.pewforum.org/. Copyright © 2009, Pew Research Center. Reproduced by permission.

As you read, consider the following questions:

1. What is Levin's opinion of the breakthrough with human skin cells acting like embryonic stem cells?

2. What is Levin's position on biotechnology?

3. What happens to views of stem cell research when placed in separate ethical and medical contexts, in Levin's opinion?

Scientists largely agree that stem cells may hold a key to the treatment, and even cure, of many serious medical conditions. But while the use of adult stem cells is widely accepted, many religious groups and others oppose stem cell research involving the use and destruction of human embryos. At the same time, many scientists say that embryonic stem cell research is necessary to unlock the promise of stem cell therapies since embryonic stem cells can develop into any cell type in the human body.

In late 2007, researchers in the United States and Japan succeeded in reprogramming adult skin cells to act like embryonic stem cells. The new development offers the possibility that the controversy over the use of embryos could end. But many scientists and supporters of embryonic stem cell research caution that this advance has not eliminated the need for embryos, at least for the time being.

[In July 2008, David Masci of] the Pew Forum sat down with Yuval Levin, author of *Tyranny of Reason*, to discuss the ethical and moral grounds for opposing embryonic stem cell research. . . .

Catching Up with the Science

David Masci: Recently, researchers in the United States and Japan successfully turned human skin cells into cells that behave like embryonic stem cells. There has been some discussion that this advance makes the moral and ethical debate over embryonic stem cells moot. Do you think that's an accurate assessment?

Yuval Levin: I think it's going to take a while for the ethical debate to catch up with the science. The scientific community has reacted very positively to this advancement, which was made in November 2007. There have been many additional scientific studies published on the topic since then, and it appears increasingly likely that the cells produced using skin cells are the equivalent of embryonic stem cells. So I think that, in time, this probably will be the final chapter of this particular debate about embryonic stem cells, but I don't think we're at the end of it quite yet.

Do you agree with Professor James Thomson, who led the American research team that made this breakthrough, when he maintains that this advance does not, for the time being, abrogate the need for embryonic stem cell research?

Part of his argument for continuing to use embryonic stem cells was backward-looking to make the point that researchers wouldn't have been able to develop this technique if they hadn't been doing embryonic stem cell research. I think that's true, although in a certain way it actually vindicates the logic of President [George W.] Bush's stem cell policy, which is to allow some work to be done—without creating an incentive for the destruction of further embryos—to advance the basic science in these kinds of directions.

Thomson also argued that there will still be a need to use embryos in the future. I think that's also a fair argument in the sense that there are always interesting things to learn from different kinds of experiments, but it doesn't address the ethical issues surrounding the debate. If there were no ethical concerns, then certainly the new development wouldn't mean embryonic research would become totally useless. But given that there *are* [ethical] concerns, the case for destroying embryos does become a lot weaker. For some people, myself included, the ethical concerns are matters of principle and don't change with new developments.

But for a lot of people, the stem cell debate has always been a matter of balance. People are aware that there are ethical concerns and that there is enormous scientific promise. Now the debate is: Given the ethical questions at stake, is the scientific promise sufficient to make us put the ethical concerns aside and support the research? I think that balance has changed because of this advance, and having an alternative to embryonic stem cell research that achieves the same result will obviously affect the way people think about the ethics of this issue.

That doesn't mean the scientists no longer have any use for embryonic stem cells or even that they won't have any use for them [in the future]. But I do think it means that people are going to change the way they reason about the balance between science and ethics because of this advance.

Intrinsic Worth

I know that you believe that human embryos have intrinsic worth. Do you believe that they have the same intrinsic worth as a five-year-old child or a 50-year-old man?

The question of intrinsic worth is complicated. I don't think it is right to try to determine an embryo's intrinsic worth by debating when human life begins. The question of when life begins is a biological question, and the answer actually is fairly straightforward: The life of an organism begins at conception. The ethical question, however, is not about when a life begins but whether every life is equal, and that's a very different question.

I think that the embryonic stem cell debate is ultimately about the question of human equality. The United States has had one answer to that question written in its "birth certificate"—the Declaration of Independence—which states that "all men are created equal." I think that examining this principle of human equality provides the right answer to this debate, but it is not a simple answer. Human equality doesn't mean that every person is the same or that every person can even be valued in the same way on every scale. What it means is that our common humanity is something that we all share. And what that means, in turn, is that we can't treat a human being in certain ways that we might non-human beings.

The protection of human life comes first. And to the extent that the debate is about whether it is acceptable to destroy a living human being for the purpose of science—even for the purpose of helping other human beings—I think that in that sense, the embryo is our equal. That doesn't mean that I would think of an embryo in the same way that I would think of a three-year-old child, but I would reject a technique that uses either of them for scientific experimentation.

So in other words, even though you would grieve the death of a 50-year-old man more than a five-day-old embryo, on at least the most basic level you believe that they both have the same right to life.

Yes, that's right. And right to life derives from human equality. The right to life is, in a way, drawn out of the political vocabulary of the Declaration of Independence. And so, to my mind, the argument at the heart of the embryonic stem cell debate is the argument about human equality.

Recently in The New Republic *magazine, Harvard psychologist Steven Pinker wrote that conservative bioethicists like yourself consistently predict the worst when looking at developments in biotechnology. He went on to say that had there been a president's council on cyber-ethics in the 1960s, "no doubt it would have decried the threat of the internet since it would inexorably lead to [a totalitarian regime like that depicted in George Orwell's novel] 1984 or computers 'taking over' like HAL in [the 1960s science fiction movie] 2001." How do you respond to this suggestion that there always seems to be this sort of chorus of doomsayers every time something new comes along?*

To my mind, biotechnology is fundamentally different from past developments in technology because it's directed to the human person. From the beginning of the scientific revolution, science and technology have tried to allow us to manipulate and shape the world around us for the benefit of man. Now that we're beginning to manipulate and shape man, the question is: For the benefit of what? In some cases that's easy to see. Obviously curing disease is more of an "old-fashioned" scientific pursuit. But there are newer scientific developments, such as certain types of human enhancement technologies that raise very complicated questions of how we should judge the ends and the means of technological advancements. That being said, Pinker has a point, in a larger sense—that judging the risks of new technologies is very difficult. In general, I think we ought to give the benefit of the doubt to our ability to use new technologies. I don't think that we should assume that the worst will happen. But there are specific instances, which are few but very important, when we do need to be cautious.

A Transcendent Standard

Let's shift gears to a question about religion and faith. Obviously there are people of faith on both sides of this debate. In fact, there are conservatives—traditional social conservatives, such as Republican Sen. Orrin Hatch of Utah—who support embryonic stem cell research. But could you explain how the Judeo-Christian and Western moral ethic informs your views on this issue and why you think that God is ultimately on your side?

Well, I don't know that I think that. My approach to this is not religious. I'm not a particularly religious person, and I come at this from more of a liberal democratic concern for human equality and the foundations of our society. That being said, those foundations are not utterly secular, and my understanding of them is not utterly secular. I think that to believe in human equality you do have to have some sense of a transcendent standard by which to make that judgment. In other words, when we talk about equality, what do we mean? Equal in relation to what?

Deliberate Deception

It is remarkable that in the debate—often carried on with little competence—the potential of *embryonic* stem cells is exaggerated in a one-sided way, while important moral questions and issues of research strategy are passed over in silence. Generally, advocates of research with embryonic stem cells use as their main argument that such research will enable us to cure all of the diseases that are incurable today—cancer, AIDS, Alzheimer's, multiple sclerosis, and so forth. Faced with such a prospect, it is supposed to be "acceptable" to "overlook" a few moral problems.

On closer inspection, however, the much extolled vision of the future turns out to be a case of completely empty promises: Given the elementary state of research today, it is by no means yet foreseeable, whether even one of the hoped-for treatments can be realized. Basically, such promised cures are a deliberate deception, for behind the mirage of a coming medical wonderland, promoted by interested parties, completely other research objectives will be pursued that are to be kept out of public discussion as much as possible.

Wolfgang Lillge,
21st Century Science & Technology,
Winter 2001–2002.

Some people have certainly tried to make a purely secular liberal argument for human equality. While I think it's very hard to ground a genuine, deep belief in human equality in a worldview that sees nothing above the material. I don't think that that belief depends on specific theological commitments. To my mind, it's an American belief more than it is a religious belief.

Certainly I think that President Bush's commitment to human equality has a lot to do with a particular Christian sense of human worth and human value. But I don't think that it's necessary to ground yourself in a particular theological or sectarian preference. I think that this is really about whether we believe in a liberal society, which comes from a belief in human equality. The American left, which for the most part is on the other side of this debate from where I am, has always been the champion of human equality, and I think that it's a question that they have to really think about.

The Pew Forum and the Pew Research Center for the People & the Press have done polling on this issue over the last six or seven years and have found that Americans generally favor embryonic stem cell research. Why do you think this has happened, and what do you think this trend indicates?

That's an interesting question. We actually did a poll here at the Ethics and Public Policy Center in February [2008] on a similar question, and the lesson I drew from that, and from some other polling that's been done, is that on the stem cell debate, people are just very confused about the facts, and the trend lines have generally followed the sense that cures are coming. In the end, the issue has been misrepresented as a choice between cures and Christianity, and people increasingly think that curing people like Christopher Reeve is just as much of a human good as protecting an embryo that they can't even imagine.

But when you dig down into people's views about stem cell research, you find a great deal of confusion, and when you put the questions in ethical terms, you find small majorities opposing it. When you put the question in medical terms, you find, I think, somewhat larger majorities supporting it. In our poll, we asked the same people a series of questions that basically put the same issue in several different ways, and their responses are total opposites of one another. The fact that the same people come out on the opposite sides of the same issue when it's put in different ways suggests to me that the issue is very hard to understand—which it is.

Frequently one hears that, ultimately, you can't stop science or "progress" and that ethical, moral and religious objections inevitably will fall by the wayside when there are clear material gains to be made. Do you think that's the most likely scenario in this case, assuming the scientific community continues to see a need for embryonic stem cell research?

Well, that's the big assumption, right? To my mind, the aim of people such as myself has always been to find ways of doing the science without violating the ethics rather than to force a choice between the science and the ethics. If we force that choice, I think it's more likely that the country would choose science over ethics, and that's exactly why we have to avoid the choice. I don't think we should be overconfident in our ability to persuade people to pass up a material benefit for an ethical principle, although I hope that can be done in the stem cell research debate. It certainly has been done in some instances when the principle was more evident and more obvious—such as imposing limits on human subject research.

Again, the aim from my point of view—and from a lot of people on my side of this argument—has been to find ways to advance the science without violating the ethics. That's the logic of President Bush's stem cell policy; that's why people have been pushing for alternatives; that's why they're encouraging the development of these latest alternatives—to avoid the choice, not to force the choice. I think that's the best thing for the country, from everybody's point of view. You don't want a situation where you've got sort of red-state medicine and blue-state medicine and people believe that the treatment their hospital is giving them is obtained in unethical ways. That would begin to break up the practice of medicine and to affect our attitudes about science—which on the whole has done a tremendous amount of good for society. So I think what everybody should aim for is finding a way to end this potentially very damaging debate rather than force a choice.

| "Open access to physician-assisted death . . . gives patients an important additional option."

Physician-Assisted Suicide Is Ethical

Timothy E. Quill

Timothy E. Quill is a professor of medical humanities, medicine, and psychiatry at the University of Rochester in New York state. In the following viewpoint, Quill contends that physician-assisted suicide can be an ethical option in cases of severe or intractable suffering. He maintains that it gives terminally ill patients a choice to escape unacceptable pain, and Oregon's legalization of the practice has improved end-of-life care while accounting for a very small, stable number of deaths. Keeping physician-assisted suicide illegal, he asserts, excludes opportunities for a second opinion, documentation, and openness among health care professionals.

As you read, consider the following questions:

1. What are the challenges in palliative care, as described by the author?

Timothy E. Quill, "Physician-Assisted Death in the United States: Are the Existing 'Last Resorts' Enough?" *Hastings Center Report*, September/October 2008. Reproduced by permission.

2. How does Quill address patients who face the scenario of future suffering?

3. What is the main risk of making physician-assisted suicide an option, in the author's opinion?

Although there has been relatively little activity in the last ten years with regard to legal access to physician-assisted death, [in fall 2008] a citizens' initiative in the state of Washington is proposing an Oregon-style law that would allow legal access to potentially lethal medication for terminally ill patients, subject to defined safeguards. As the rhetoric inevitably heats up, this seems like a good time to review areas of progress in palliative [pain-relieving] and end-of-life care and to consider whether laws like the one on the table in Washington are either needed or desirable. [Voters approved the initiave in November 2008.]

Several things are clear: (1) Palliative care and hospice have improved in terms of access and delivery, and they remain the standards of care for addressing the suffering of seriously ill patients. (2) Despite state-of-the-art palliative measures, there will remain a relatively small number of patients whose suffering is insufficiently relieved. (3) Several "last resort" options, including aggressive pain management, forgoing life-sustaining therapies, voluntarily stopping eating and drinking, and sedation to unconsciousness to relieve otherwise intractable suffering, could address many of these cases. The question remains as to whether physician-assisted death—that is, providing terminally ill patients with a potentially lethal prescription that they could ingest on their own to relieve otherwise intractable suffering by directly hastening death—should be one of these last-resort options.

My own answer to this last question is a cautious "yes": open access to physician-assisted death, subject to the safeguards of excellent palliative care and access to other last-resort options, gives patients an important additional option, and the benefits of legalization outweigh the risks.

Progress in the Last Decade

Perhaps the most dramatic sign of progress has been the coming of age of the palliative care movement, which allows fully informed decision-making and the provision of treatments to maximize quality of life for all seriously ill patients alongside any and all disease-directed treatment that patients want to continue. Almost all major medical centers now have inpatient palliative care consultation services, and similar services are spreading into community hospitals. Consultation possibilities are also spreading into the outpatient and home settings, although the gaps between need and availability are much wider in these contexts. The American Board of Medical Specialties has recently given palliative care the status of being a board-certified subspecialty, and fellowship programs are sprouting up across the country.

There remain serious challenges. There are not enough skilled palliative care clinicians to meet the growing needs, and reimbursement for palliative care services—which rely heavily on counseling and coordination of care rather than expensive procedures—remains problematic. Similar gaps exist in providing basic palliative care education for all clinicians who care for seriously ill patients, and in generating an evidence base for the field. Nonetheless, palliative care seems to have passed the "tipping point" as a field; most patients and families can find the treatments that they need regardless of their stage of disease.

When patients become terminally ill, access to palliative care is facilitated by the proliferation of hospice programs. Hospice remains our premiere program to provide palliative care for terminally ill patients who are willing to forgo further treatment of their underlying disease, as it provides, pays for, and coordinates comprehensive quality-of-life-oriented treatments for terminally ill patients. Hospice has expanded considerably in the last ten years, primarily in two domains: the inclusion of terminally ill patients with diseases other than cancer—congestive heart failure, dementia, and chronic lung disease, for example—and the ability to supplement the palliative aspects of care for terminally ill patients who reside in skilled nursing homes.

Despite this progress, the majority of patients who die in the United States are never transitioned to hospice, mostly because of a requirement that once they are in hospice they will forgo disease-directed therapy. Some larger hospices are experimenting with loosening these restrictions through "bridge" programs that let patients continue active treatments that are important to them and have some potential for helping while at the same time receiving the full benefits of hospice. Since hospices are paid on a per diem basis (on average, about $135 per day), only the very large, affluent hospices can afford to offer expensive disease-directed therapy at the same time that they are providing and paying for comprehensive palliative care, but there is much more flexibility and willingness to experiment with these areas now than ten years ago.

Significant progress has also been made in the articulation and provision of last-resort options for patients whose suffering becomes unacceptable to them despite state-of-the-art palliative care. Ten years ago, the problem of intractable suffering was often not acknowledged or was blamed on the clinician ("They don't have adequate expertise") or the patients ("They want too much control over their fate"). Now, it is much more widely acknowledged that even with the best possible palliative care, there will always be a small percentage of cases where suffering sometimes becomes unacceptably severe, and that clinicians are obligated to treat these circumstances as a palliative care emergency that requires consultation and committed efforts to respond in the most helpful, least harmful way. . . .

The Empirical Data

By far the best data about physician-assisted death in the United States come from Oregon, where the practice is reported to the health department and where annual summaries have been prepared every year since legalization. The practice has been remarkably stable over the ten intervening years, accounting for approximately one out of every thousand deaths per year. This appears to be a very small number given the amount of controversy surrounding the practice, but one in fifty patients talk to their doctor about it, and one in six talk with family members, suggesting that the *availability* of such an escape may be much more important to many patients than its actual use. The Oregon statute requires that patients be informed of "feasible alternatives," including hospice and palliative care and other last resort alternatives, and some choose alternatives other than physician-assisted death.

There are also data from Oregon to suggest that the legalization of physician-assisted death enhances rather than undermines other aspects of palliative and end-of-life care. Oregon has one of the highest rates of hospice referral in the nation, and the vast majority of patients who choose physician-assisted death are simultaneously enrolled in hospice. Oregon also has relatively high rates of opioid prescription per capita, and physicians as well as other medical professionals have very high rates of attending training courses in both palliative care and end-of-life medical decision-making. There is also a statewide form, "Physician Orders for Life-Sustaining Treatment" (POLST), for recording a patient's wishes about cardiopulmonary resuscitation and other potentially life-sustaining therapies. The form has become a model for other states. Overall, Oregon appears to be among the leaders in comparison to other states in virtually all aspects of palliative and end-of-life care, including allowing open access to physician-assisted death, subject to safeguards.

The secret practice of physician-assisted death in the rest of the nation is very difficult to study. To admit to participation, a physician has to admit to a crime, and along with any family present, runs the risk of prosecution. On the other hand, there appears to be very little interest in prosecuting such cases providing they are not discovered or flaunted, leading to a "don't ask, don't tell" policy that is unpredictable and potentially dangerous. Under this policy, there is no opportunity to get second opinions from experts in palliative care, no documentation, and considerable potential for idiosyncratic responses from clinicians.

In the mid-1990s, I was part of a team that conducted an empirical study of the secret practice, using research techniques that protected anonymity. We found that physician-assisted death and euthanasia accounted for approximately 1 to 2 percent of deaths. Although this appears to be ten to twenty times higher than the rates reported in Oregon, the reporting techniques were so different that the rates are not directly comparable. On the other hand, we know from Oregon that conversations with doctors about these issues are common, and it appears to be much better and safer to have the conversations out in the open rather than in secret.

Very little is known about the frequency of other last resort practices in the United States. Data from the Netherlands, where all end-of-life practices are regularly studied, suggest that forgoing life-sustaining therapy and prescribing "opioids in large doses" are each reported to account for approximately 20 percent of deaths, which fits with my clinical experience in the United States. There are no reliable data about the frequency of voluntarily stopping eating and drinking [VSED] in the United States, although the practice is thought to be rare. In our two hospice programs in Rochester, New York, where VSED is permitted and supported as a last resort, it accounts for less than 1 percent of deaths. Sedation to unconsciousness to treat otherwise intractable physical symptoms appears to be used very variably in the United States, apparently depending more on the values and practice patterns of the practitioners than of the patients. Reports vary from no deaths to half of all deaths, depending in part on definitions but also on practice patterns. At our hospital, where sedation to unconsciousness for treatment of intractable symptoms is subject to guidelines and restrictions that include a mandatory palliative care consult, it accounts for less than 1 percent of deaths.

The Clinical Context

All last-resort options, including physician-assisted death, make sense only if excellent palliative care is already being provided. Mandatory palliative care consultation should therefore be a standard safeguard for any and all of these practices. Over the *next* ten years, medical institutions and professional groups should ensure that all clinicians who care for seriously ill patients are competent in the basics of palliative care and that specialty-based palliative care consultation is available for the more challenging cases.

There is also a need to develop explicit, predictable strategies to respond to difficult clinical situations where patients experience severe suffering despite state-of-the-art palliative care. Many of these patients will benefit from a discussion and exploration of last-resort options that may or may not include physician-assisted death. There are two main clinical situations in which this might come up:

Patients who are worried about future suffering and wonder what options would be available to them. This conversation begins with an exploration about hopes, fears, and prior experiences of family and friends. Such patients frequently want to know what options they could have in the future if their suffering becomes unacceptable to them. In response to these inquiries, the clinician should talk to the patient about how he or she approaches such situations and what last-resort options could be provided if needed. Many patients are reassured by learning about options other than physician-assisted death and by the willingness of the clinician to explore this domain and to commit to working with them and addressing their suffering throughout the illness until death. They can then be free to spend their remaining time and energy on other important personal and family matters.

Patients who eventually experience suffering that is unacceptable to them. This is a much smaller population than those who are worried about the future, but these patients' needs can be more challenging. The starting point is always to explore the patient's suffering in its totality, including why it is now experienced as unacceptable. Part of this assessment is to ensure that standard palliative care is being skillfully applied, and that the request does not emanate from anxiety or depression that might be otherwise addressed. A second opinion by a specialist in palliative care should be obtained. If there are no good alternatives, then the last-resort options that are legally available should be explored in the approximate order presented in this [viewpoint]. Usually, but not always, options other than physician-assisted death will adequately address the patient's clinical situation and be acceptable to the patient. In the event that no other possibilities are workable or acceptable, physician-assisted death would need to be considered in light of the legal environment (the approach in Oregon will be very different than the rest of the country) and the values of patient, family, and clinician.

Will Physician-Assisted Death Be Necessary?

Some patients will prefer access to physician-assisted death even if the other last-resort options are predictably available. Patients who request and eventually act using physician-assisted death in Oregon have a strong interest in controlling their fate, and physician-assisted death puts more choice directly in their hands. However, all the last-resort options, including physician-assisted death, are imperfect. Although each addresses some situations particularly well, there are other situations where they would not be as helpful.

For example, voluntarily stopping eating and drinking has the advantage of putting the decision in the patient's hands, but it requires tremendous discipline not to drink if one is thirsty and capable of drinking, and the duration of the process is too long if symptoms are severe and immediate. On the other hand, medical sedation to unconsciousness may be very frightening to those who value consciousness and being in charge, and there is no way to verify that the sedated patient is not still suffering but unable to report it. Finally, physician-assisted death requires that the patient be physically capable of self-administration and able to swallow a concentrated amount of lethal medication. In addition to these practical issues, any of these options may be morally troubling for patient, family, physician, or staff.

Adding physician-assisted death to the list of last-resort options has both risks and benefits. One benefit is that it adds another important possibility for terminally ill patients who experience unacceptable suffering. We should be as responsive as possible to these patients without violating fundamental values, but it is clear that the patient's values in this context count the most, followed by the family and then the clinician (if the course of action requires the physician's participation). Most patients will be reassured by the possibility of an escape, and the vast majority will never need to activate that possibility. But some patients will need a way out, and arbitrarily withholding one important option from patients whose options are so limited seems unfair.

The main risk of including physician-assisted death with other last-resort options is that it seems to be very polarizing in the United States, where there is wide agreement about palliative care and hospice being the standards of care and also a surprising level of acceptance of the other last resort possibili-

It's About Patients

Physician-assisted suicide isn't about physicians becoming killers. It's about patients whose suffering we can't relieve, and about not turning away from them when they ask for help. Will there be physicians who feel they can't do this? Of course, and they shouldn't be obliged to. But if other physicians consider it merciful to help such patients by merely writing a prescription, it is unreasonable to place them in jeopardy of criminal prosecution, loss of license, or other penalty for doing so.

Peter Rogatz, Humanist, *November/December 2001.*

ties. Even the Supreme Court, in its 1997 decision, made it clear that "obtaining medication . . . to alleviate suffering even to the point of causing unconsciousness and hastening death" is legally acceptable. Opponents of physician-assisted death may work to further restrict access or even prohibit access to other last resort alternatives as they become more well known and predictably available.

On the Horizon

It seems highly likely that palliative care and hospice will continue to expand in the United States and other Western countries. There are very few places in the health care system where we can simultaneously save money and improve quality, but palliative care and hospice have the potential to do both. On the quality side, improvements in pain and symptom management, more informed medical decision-making, and enhanced patient and family support are core elements of palliative care and hospice. The cost savings will come not from restricting access to expensive treatments and technologies, but from a better informed consent process for patients and families concerning medical treatments with marginal benefit and coordinated care for patients with very complex treatment. Hospice continues to be the gold standard for end-of-life care, but its challenge is to design programs that would allow patients to simultaneously continue some disease-directed therapies in order to serve a wider range of dying patients. If these programs can be proven cost-effective, then perhaps the hospice benefit can be expanded, and hospice and palliative care could be better integrated into traditional medical care. Palliative care needs to be part of the standard of care for all seriously ill patients, whether or not they choose to continue disease-directed therapy in any form.

The last-resort options other than physician-assisted death must become more standardized, available, and accountable. There is currently too much variation. Some patients may be denied access to them because clinicians or institutions are reluctant to use them, while at the same time, others are given last-resort options when more standard palliative measures would have been more appropriate. Better policies and procedures should begin at the national level, with local programs following suit. Fortunately, medicine seems to be moving in this direction. Witness a recently published American Medical Association guideline on sedation to unconsciousness that is consistent with position statements by the American Academy of Hospice and Palliative Medicine and others.

Similar guidelines and policies are needed for voluntarily stopping eating and drinking. Because these options are intended to be rarely used, all institutions should review their own practices against the position statements of leadership organizations. For example, my institution has a guideline on sedation to unconsciousness for treatment of refractory suffering, and we review every single case in which it is utilized. The state of California is considering a law entitled the California Right to Know End-of-Life Options Act, which requires that patients be given information about both hospice and last-resort options, should they request it. The goal of all these initiatives is to improve predictable access and accountability both for hospice/palliative care and for legally permitted last-resort options.

In the domain of physician-assisted death, the most pressing change on the horizon is the Oregon-style citizens' initiative in the state of Washington. Residents of the state are already relatively well educated on the subject, having been through an unsuccessful initiative in 1991, and they are more aware of the Oregon experience, being adjacent geographically and relatively similar demographically. Citizens' initiatives begin by gathering signatures of support from a large number of residents. If the legally determined threshold is achieved, the initiative is then placed on the ballot during the next election cycle and subject to the popular vote. Not all states sanction citizens' initiatives, but in my opinion, they are more likely to be successful in legalizing physician-assisted death than legislative approaches, given the relatively high level of public support and the tendency for the issue to get polarized in legislative situations. Nonetheless, legislative processes to legalize physician-assisted death were recently attempted in California, and before that there were near misses in Hawaii and New Hampshire.

Although some proponents of physician-assisted death will find the incremental, state-by-state approach to legalization frustrating, it has some value. For one thing, it gives us time to study the intended and unintended effects of legalization before national implementation. We can simultaneously evaluate the impact of better and more widespread access to hospice and palliative care, and of more predictable and accountable availability of other last-resort options. In addition, it keeps the movement a grass-roots one—particularly when it happens through citizens' initiatives. That may not make the practice of physician-assisted death less controversial, but it can perhaps make the process through which physician-assisted death is legalized less controversial.

> *"None of the . . . three (suicide, assisted suicide or euthanasia) has any moral justification in the light of sound reason and/or medical science."*

Physician-Assisted Suicide Is Unethical

Peter C. Glover

In the following viewpoint, Peter C. Glover contends that physician-assisted suicide cannot be ethically justified. He offers several arguments against physician-assisted suicide: it is a patient's cry for help or sign of depression, suicidal intent is temporary, pain can be controlled, and legalizing the practice in any form will lead to involuntary euthanasia. Permitting physician-assisted suicide in a society, the author states, would create a culture where a life can be judged as a burden and not worth living. Glover is a writer based in Colchester, England, and the author of numerous books, including The Politics of Faith: Essays on the Morality of Key Current Issues.

As you read, consider the following questions:

1. What does the term "passive euthanasia" mean to the author?

Peter C. Glover, "Euthanasia: Can It Ever Be Right to Legalise It?" *Catholic Insight*, vol. 17, February 2009, pp. 8–9. Copyright 2009 Catholic Insight. Reproduced by permission.

2. How does Glover back his claim that pain for seriously ill patients is manageable?

3. How does Herbert Hendin, as cited by the author, respond to the assertion that physician-assisted suicide empowers patients?

For two millennia the Hippocratic tradition has stood for the "sanctity" of human life. We can alleviate the unbearable in life better than ever before. We can do that and not eliminate life itself . . . medicine cannot be both our healer and our killer.

—C. Everett Koop,
Former Surgeon General of the United States

The courts in the English-speaking world have recently witnessed a number of high-profile and distressing cases where individuals have argued both for the 'right to die' and even the 'right to live' in the event of incapacitation. But it was perhaps in the troubling case of the young American woman Terri Schiavo that the issues surrounding euthanasia have been most hotly debated.[1] This was a case that, like no other, split the conscience of a nation, causing a public debate which cut deep into the American psyche and exposed the core ethical arguments surrounding the whole morality of euthanasia or assisted suicide as never before.

At the heart of the debate was not only the 'human right' to choose death, but the 'right' for society, in general, to be complicit in its acquiescence, hence legally.

Clarifying Our Terms

Before we get to grips with the issue itself however, it is important, if we wish to avoid the confusion that often derails genuine debate, to clarify our terminology.

1. Schiavo was in a persistent vegetative state for several years in Florida. Her husband petitioned the courts to allow her feeding tube to be disconnected, but he faced legal challenges from her parents. In 2005, Schiavo was removed from life support and died.

1. Suicide—is self-killing, some would say self-murder.

2. Assisted suicide—involves enlisting the aid of another person, often a doctor, to end one's own life. Those 'assisting' provide the means of death but do not take part in the killing directly.

3. Euthanasia—occurs when someone other than the 'patient'—a doctor, nurse or someone else—performs an action, such as a lethal injection, which brings about death.

4. Passive euthanasia—occurs when the withdrawal of medical assistance or life-sustaining treatment leads 'naturally' to the death of the patient. This term is seldom used because of the near universal agreement that it is, and has always been, a justifiable treatment ethically (i.e. allowing 'nature' to take its course).

The Heart of the Matter

Let me state my case here bluntly: with the exception of no. 4, which has been largely unquestioned common medical practice for centuries, none of the other three (suicide, assisted suicide or euthanasia) has any moral justification in the light of sound reason and/or medical science.

I am opposed to euthanasia in all its forms, not just because I, as a Christian, believe the Creator God is demonstrably opposed to it, making no provision for it in His revealed will to mankind and through the teaching of the Catholic Church, but also because the biblical and Church teaching, which is not the subject of this particular article, is wholly supported by every ethical, philosophical and reasoned argument available. I mention my biblical worldview here with good reason. All too often, the issue of worldview is obscured in the public debate. Indeed, many Christians even feel it judicious not to mention it at all, as if the assumption is that the secular person, unlike the Christian, does not possess a 'worldview' or cultural or philosophical spectacles through which he views the world. Nothing could be further from the truth! It is just a case of articulating what one's worldview is, and how it affects and underpins the views or opinions being expressed.

This is no secondary matter whenever any moral issue is being discussed. When all is said and done, the Judeo-Christian worldview is a well-reasoned pattern of belief in which the sanctity of life is given moral substance. Those who criticise such a worldview ought to be called upon to articulate and uphold their own.

The advantage here is that we can point to a 'gold standard' of moral right or wrong—in fact the moral gold standard which is the foundation of Western civilization's Judeo-Christian heritage. Those who hold secular and liberal privatised worldviews often struggle to sustain them. While the biblical and conservative worldview is focused on the higher good of the community, one usually finds that the secular liberal focuses on the rights of the individual. The reality is, however, that one must outweigh the other. And the Bible as well as historic tradition dictates that it must be the higher good of the community that wins out.

Having made this important point however, in this article I intend to equip the ordinary Catholic Christian with insight into the case against the legalisation of euthanasia from a secular perspective to reinforce the biblical argument.

Matters of Mind and Body

Here, in a nutshell, are the very practical and key arguments against legalising euthanasia/assisted suicide in any form:

1. A request for assisted suicide is typically a cry for help. In reality it is typically a call for counselling, assistance and positive alternatives as solutions to very real problems.

2. Suicidal intent is typically transient. Of those who attempt suicide, fewer than 4% go on to kill themselves in the next five years; less than 11% will commit suicide over the next 35 years.

3. Terminally ill patients who desire death are typically depressed—and depression is treatable. In one study, 24% of those desiring death had clinical depression.

4. Pain is controllable. The array of treatments to control pain (palliative care) is vast and impressive today. Often the person seeking death does not need assistance to commit suicide but a doctor better trained in palliative care. The Nightingale Alliance states that 95% of all pain is controllable and the other 5% can be reduced to a tolerable level.

5. Legalising voluntary euthanasia almost always means legalising non-voluntary euthanasia. In America, for instance, state courts have consistently ruled that if competent people have a right, then incompetent people must be 'given' the same 'right.' It is highly likely that the British courts would rule the same way.

6. The Netherlands' experience in legalising voluntary assisted suicide for those with terminal illness has spread to include non-voluntary euthanasia for people with no terminal illness. Half of the killings in the Netherlands are now non-voluntary and a 'culture of death,' admitted as such privately by many Dutch doctors, has now taken root there. It has become a common legal 'solution' for those with mental illness, permanent disability, and even old age.

7. You don't solve problems by getting rid of the people to whom the problems happen. The more difficult but humane solution to human suffering is to address the problem, not get rid of the human.

The Ultimate Patient Abandonment

Legalizing physician-assisted suicide strikes at the heart of what we do as physicians and adds ambiguity to the physician-patient relationship. The physician's primary directive is to *first, do no harm*. Physician-assisted suicide destroys the trust between the patient and doctor. Under the pretense of providing compassion, the physician is relieved of his or her primary responsibility to the patient—to safeguard life and to provide comfort to the suffering. It is the ultimate patient abandonment.

Association of Northern California Oncologists and Medical Oncology Association of Southern California,
Position Statement on Physician-Assisted Suicide and Opposition to AB374 *April 16, 2007.*

The Dutch Experience

The oft-cited experience of legalised euthanasia in the Netherlands is also worth closer scrutiny than is usually the case. Herbert Hendin, MD, Executive Director of the American Suicide Foundation and Professor of Psychiatry at New York Medical College, has written the following authoritative analysis of euthanasia in the Netherlands in his *Seduced By Death: Doctors, Patients and the Dutch Cure.* Here are some key quotes:

"The doctors who help set Dutch euthanasia policies are aware that euthanasia is basically out of control in the Netherlands. They admitted this to me privately. Yet in their public statements and articles they maintain there are no serious problems. . . ." p. 14

"The experience of the Dutch people makes it clear that legalisation of assisted suicide and euthanasia is not the answer to the problems of people who are terminally ill. The Netherlands has moved from assisted suicide to euthanasia, from euthanasia for people who are terminally ill to euthanasia for people who are chronically ill, from euthanasia for physical illnesses to euthanasia for psychological distress, and from voluntary euthanasia to involuntary euthanasia (called "termination of the patient without explicit request"). The Dutch government's own commissioned research has documented that in more than one thousand cases a year, doctors actively cause or hasten death without the patient's request." p. 23

"Virtually every guideline established by the Dutch to regulate euthanasia has been modified or violated with impunity." p. 23

"In the selling of assisted suicide and euthanasia, words like 'empowerment' and 'dignity' are associated with the choice for dying. But who is being empowered? The more one knows about individual cases, the more apparent it becomes that needs other than those of the patient often prevail. Empowerment flows towards the relatives, the doctor who offers a speedy way out if he cannot offer a cure, or the activists who have found in death a cause that gives meaning to their own lives. The patient who may have asked to die in the hope of receiving emotional reassurance that all around her want her to live, may find that ... she has set in motion a process whose momentum she cannot control." pp. 43–4.

A Culture of Death

In short, there are no scientific, medical or ethical reasons why any of us, not just Catholic Christians, should condone or support the legalisation of euthanasia in society.

No one can prevent someone, intent on the act, from taking out a revolver and blowing his brains out, or administering a lethal dose of drugs to himself or another. But that is not the issue here.

The issue here is whether there are sound reasons why a society and a nation should acquiesce in the process by legalising it. If we are intent on protecting the weak and retaining our current culture of life, in the Hippocratic tradition, then we must face whether we would rather introduce a culture of uncertainty and of death as has happened in the Netherlands. A culture where we can never be sure whether someone, somewhere, believes that our 'quality of life' is such that the world—according to their worldview—would be better off without us or those we love, brings dreadful uncertainty and immense unnecessary suffering.

"No man has power to retain the spirit, or power over the day of death" Ecclesiastes 8:8 (ESV).

"I don't believe that we should be so quick to greet cloning technology with a permanent injunction."

Cloning Is Ethical

Jacob M. Appel

Jacob M. Appel is a bioethicist and medical historian. He also writes fiction that explores biomedical ethics. In the following viewpoint, Appel argues that the promises of human cloning should not be dismissed and deserve an unbiased evaluation. While the potential of birth defects and long-term health complications currently remains high, the author insists that human cloning is inevitable and thus laws and safeguards must be set in place to protect children born through the procedure. Appel contends that research and efforts for human cloning should not be stopped, but must proceed with caution.

As you read, consider the following questions:

1. Why does Appel question President Barack Obama's position on human cloning?

2. How does the author view cloning children for organ donation?

Jacob M. Appel, "Should We Really Fear Reproductive Human Cloning?" *Huffington Post*, April 6, 2009. Reproduced by permission.

3. What is Appel's opinion of parents cloning a child who has died?

In his remarks lifting the ban on the federal funding of embryonic stem cell research [in March 2009], President [Barack] Obama took pains to distinguish research cloning from reproductive cloning. According to the President, "the use of cloning for human reproduction" is "dangerous, profoundly wrong, and has no place in our society, or any society," and he promised to ensure that "our government never opens the door" to such a practice. What the President did not do was to explain precisely why he opposes reproductive cloning. Is his opposition solely based upon the health risks that cloning techniques, such as somatic cell nuclear transfer, may impose upon children born as a result of this novel technology? Or does he believe that human reproductive cloning ought to be prohibited even if it could someday be rendered as safe—or safer—than other forms of procreation? To some who oppose reproductive cloning, as polls consistently suggest that a majority of Americans still do, these questions may seem purely academic: As long as our society adopts the right policy, one might argue, why concern ourselves with whether we are doing so for the wrong reasons or even for conflicting reasons? The reality of the legislative debates preceding state cloning bans—from California's 1997 prohibition to the statute enacted [in April 2009] in Montana—is that much antagonism to reproductive cloning appears to reflect an inchoate, emotional and often illogical repugnance to the practice on the part of lawmakers, rather than well-reasoned and well-articulated opposition. What is actually needed is an unbiased assessment of both the perils and promises of cloning humans.

Most evidence suggests [that] reproductive human cloning, at the present time, would pose serious dangers to any children so produced. The frequency of birth defects and long-term health complications in cloned animals remains exceedingly high. These genetic disorders likely result from programming errors due to what biologists call "imprinting," and arise when the double sets of maternally- or paternally-derived genes in the embryo "speak" simultaneously. While scientists are currently working on reprogramming techniques, which would prevent these errors, the feasibility of such efforts remains largely uncertain. What is far clearer is that, if society's only objection to reproductive cloning is the danger that the technology poses to the offspring, then research to render human cloning safe should be pursued vigorously.

The most obvious benefit of reproductive cloning—if it could be rendered safe—would be as a source of transplantable tissues and organs. I certainly do not mean to suggest that cloned children would have any fewer human rights or should be treated any differently than non-cloned children. Quite the contrary: Much as children conceived in "test tubes" are morally and legally indistinguishable from children conceived in utero, any moral approach to reproductive cloning would ensure that clones were treated with the same respect and dignity as any other identical twins. However, parents frequently decide to produce additional offspring in order to provide matching bone-marrow donors for their critically-ill children. Pediatric kidney donations between living siblings takes place in many nations. For a family with a dying child, the prospect of using cloning to create a potential donor with a set of perfectly-matched genes—and ultimately, two healthy, lovable children—might be a godsend. The ethics surrounding such procedures are highly complex. Nobody should believe otherwise. However, one should never mistake the complexity of making a decision for its underlying morality. Certainly, there is a wide difference between believing that the possibilities of human cloning should be approached with wisdom and considerable caution, as do I, and deciding a priori that such potentially therapeutic opportunities should be dismissed out of hand. I cannot imagine that President Obama's re-

Two People, One Soul?

But what of the souls? Can two people share the one soul? Is it not wrong to force two personalities on to one piece of divine substance? Again, the fact that there are identical twins counts against there being a problem. Twins seem to manage, and that seems to suggest that each person is able to be ensouled regardless of their genetic make-up. That is, assuming souls exist at all. These days theologians don't make a big thing of the soul. But even if there are souls, it seems unlikely to count against cloning. It's hard to imagine that God would have any difficulty telling the difference between one clone and another.

Colin Honey, The Age, *January 1, 2003.*

marks were intended to mean that, if reproductive cloning could be rendered safe for both mother and baby, and if it could save the life of a desperate sibling, it would still be profoundly wrong.

Only a Matter of Time

Individuals may wish to clone children for many additional reasons: some that strike mainstream society as highly reasonable, others that strike us as rather peculiar. Infertile couples might use the technology to produce children with some of their own DNA. A family who has lost a child in an accident might find some solace in cloning their lost son or daughter; the second kid would, of course, be a distinct human being from the first, with its own identity, but the sense of continuity experienced by the mourning parents might provide comfort nonetheless. The Raëlian Church has pursued cloning technology for religious purposes. As long as a scientific consensus exists that cloning is a health threat to the offspring, these individuals should not be permitted to risk bringing a severely disabled child into the world. I think most reasonable people would agree that when the health of children is at stake, we should set the safety bar high and take few unnecessary risks. However, if the time comes when scientists conclude that reproductive cloning can be conducted without a threat to the health of the offspring, then the burden will fall upon opponents to explain precisely why such a practice threatens human dignity or societal welfare. The cry of "we don't like it"—which has been used to justify opposing every aspect of human enlightenment from women's suffrage to gay equality—will simply not be a sufficient answer.

What has been lost in the rush to condemn reproductive cloning wholesale has been any meaningful effort to protect future children created through such a procedure. Whether the practice is legal or not in the United States, it will likely be only a matter of time before some determined scientist, somewhere in the world, creates a cloned human being. We need clear laws to establish the relationship between the supplier of the cloned DNA and the resulting progeny (e.g. Are they siblings? Parent and child? What are the clone's inheritance rights?) We require guarantees that, if genetic defects do arise in such children as a result of cloning, treatment for these conditions will be covered by private health insurance. And we need careful regulation and funding to ensure that the procedure is rendered safe—if that can be done—before cloned embryos are brought to term. In short, we need legislation to ensure that any future cloned men and women will be treated with the dignity and humanity that they deserve.

In an ideal world, human reproductive cloning would be safe, legal and rare. I say rare because my guess is that the majority of people, myself included, would have little desire to raise cloned offspring. After all, it is now possible to clone pets—but few of us would choose to spend a spare $150,000 on such a venture. Yet thirty-eight years after James Watson's seminal essay, "Moving Toward the Clonal Man," called for increased public debate on this promising and perplexing subject, I don't believe that we should be so quick to greet cloning technology with a permanent injunction. Instead, what human reproductive cloning requires at the moment is a yellow light, telling us to proceed with extreme caution, until we know with confidence whether the technology can ever be used to produce healthy babies.

| *"The ban [on cloning] deserves the support of all."*

Cloning Is Unethical

Leon R. Kass

Leon R. Kass is Harding Professor of Social Thought at the University of Chicago and former chairman of the President's Council on Bioethics. In the following viewpoint, Kass writes that human cloning is an unethical practice. The duplication and destruction of embryos—even for medical good—violates the sanctity of life, he argues. Moreover, he alleges that reproductive cloning robs children of the right to descend from a mother and father and paves the way to "manufactured" babies. And with advancements in stem cell research that do away with the need for embryos altogether, therapeutic cloning is no longer justified, he maintains.

As you read, consider the following questions:

1. How does the author describe the arguments for therapeutic cloning?

2. How have scientists worked their way around therapeutic cloning, as stated by Kass?

3. What does the author recommend in his proposed ban against reproductive cloning?

In his [2008] State of the Union address President [George W.] Bush spoke briefly on matters of life and science. He stated his intention to expand funding for new possibilities in medical research, to take full advantage of recent break-throughs in stem cell research that provide pluripotent stem cells without destroying nascent human life. At the same time, he continued, "we must also ensure that all life is treated with the dignity that it deserves. And so I call on Congress to pass legislation that bans unethical practices such as the buying, selling, patenting, or cloning of human life."

As in his previous State of the Union addresses, the president's call for a ban on human cloning was greeted by considerable applause from both sides of the aisle. But Congress has so far failed to pass any anti-cloning legislation, and unless a new approach is adopted, it will almost certainly fail again.

Fortunately, new developments in stem cell research suggest a route to effective and sensible anti-cloning legislation, exactly at a time when novel success in cloning human embryos makes such legislation urgent. Until now, the cloning debate has been hopelessly entangled with the stem cell debate, where the friends and the enemies of embryonic stem cell research have managed to produce a legislative stalemate on cloning. The new scientific findings make it feasible to dis-entangle these matters and thus to forge a successful legislative strategy. To see how this can work, we need first to review the past attempts and the reasons they failed.

Three Important Values

Three important values, differently weighted by the contending sides, were (and are) at issue in the debates about cloning and embryonic stem cells: scientific and medical progress, the sanctity of human life, and human dignity. We seek to cure disease and relieve suffering through vigorous research, conducted within acceptable moral boundaries. We seek to protect vulnerable human life against destruction and exploitation. We seek to defend human procreation against degrading reproductive practices—such as cloning or embryo fusing—that would deny children their due descent from one father and one mother and their right not to be "manufactured."

Embryonic stem cell research pits the first value against the second. Many upholders of the sanctity of human life regard embryo destruction as unethical even if medical good may come of it; many partisans of medical research, denying to nascent human life the same respect they give to life after birth, regard cures for disease as morally imperative even if moral harm may come of it. But the deepest challenge posed by cloning has to do not with saving life or avoiding death, but with human dignity, and the cloning issue is therefore only accidentally bound up with the battle about stem cell research. Yet both parties to the stem cell debate happily turned the cloning controversy into the life controversy.

The faction favoring embryonic stem cell research wanted to clone embryos for biomedical research, and touted cloning's potential to produce individualized (that is, rejection-proof) stem cells that might eventually be used for therapy. Its proposed anti-cloning legislation (the Kennedy-Feinstein-Hatch bill) would ban only "reproductive cloning" (cloning to produce children) while endorsing the creation of cloned human embryos for research. Such cloning-for-biomedical-research its proponents originally called "therapeutic cloning," hoping that the goal of "therapy" would get people to overcome their repugnance for "cloning." But when that strategy backfired, they disingenuously denied that the cloning of embryos for research is really cloning (they now call it, after the technique used to clone, SCNT, somatic cell nuclear transfer). They also denied that the product is a human embryo. These Orwellian [like the "doublespeak" of the totalitarian government described in George Orwell's *1984*] tactics succeeded in confusing many legislators and the larger public.

The faction opposed to embryonic stem cell research wanted to safeguard nascent human life. Its proposed anti-cloning legislation (the Weldon-Stupak bill in the House, the Brownback-Landrieu bill in the Senate) would ban all human cloning—both for reproduction and for biomedical research—by banning the initial step, the creation of cloned human embryos. (This is the approach I have favored, largely because I thought it the most effective way to prevent the production of cloned children.) But most of the bill's pro-life supporters cared much more that embryos not be created and sacrificed than that children not be clones. Accordingly, they sought to exploit the public's known opposition to cloning babies to gain a beachhead against creating embryos for destructive research, which practice, although ineligible for federal funding, has never been illegal in the United States. Initially, this strategy worked: In the summer of 2001, the Weldon-Stupak bill passed the House by a large bipartisan majority. (It has been passed again several times since.) But momentum was lost in the Senate, owing to delays caused by [the terrorist attacks of] 9/11 and strong lobbying by the pro-stem cell forces, after which time an impasse was reached, neither side being able to gain enough votes to close debate. . . .

Another Chance to Act

Fast forward to 2008. We are in the last year of the Bush presidency. Despite the president's numerous calls for action, we remain the only major nation in the high-tech world that cannot summon itself to ban human cloning, thanks to the standoff over the embryo issues. Fortunately, science has given Congress another chance to act. In the last six months, the scientific landscape has changed dramatically. On the one

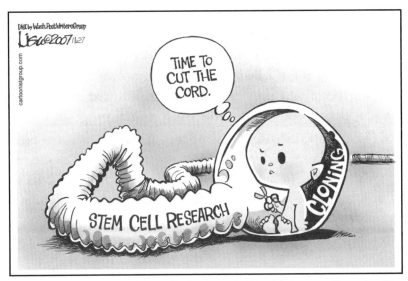

Lisa Benson, "Time to Cut the Cord." Lisa Benson's Editorial Cartoons, November 27, 2007.

hand, the need for anti-cloning legislation is now greater than ever; on the other hand, there are reasons why a new approach can succeed.

Here is what's new. After the 2005 Korean reports of the cloning of human embryos turned out to be a fraud, many said that human cloning could not be achieved. Yet late in 2007 Oregon scientists succeeded for the first time in cloning primate embryos and growing them to the blastocyst (5-7–day) stage, and then deriving embryonic stem cells from them. More recently, other American scientists, using the Oregon technique, have reported the creation of cloned human embryos. The age of human cloning is here, and the first clones, alas, do not read "made in China."

On the stem cell front, the news is decidedly better. In the last two years, several laboratories have devised methods of obtaining pluripotent human stem cells (the functional equivalent of embryonic stem cells) without the need to destroy embryos. The most remarkable and most promising of these approaches was reported by both Japanese and American scientists (including Jamie Thompson, the discoverer of human embryonic stem cells). It is the formation of human (induced) pluripotent stem cells (iPSCs) by means of the re-programming (also called de-differentiation) of somatic cells. Mature, specialized skin cells have been induced to revert to the pluripotent condition of their originating progenitor.

The therapeutic usefulness of this approach has also been newly demonstrated, by the successful treatment of sickle cell anemia in mice. Some iPSCs were derived from skin cells of an afflicted mouse; the sickle cell genetic defect in these iPSCs was corrected; the treated iPSCs were converted into blood-forming stem cells; and the now-normal blood-forming stem cells were transferred back into the afflicted mouse, curing the disease.

Scientists have hailed these results. All parties to the stem cell debates have noted that the embryonic-stem-cell war may soon be over, inasmuch as science has found a morally un-problematic way to obtain the desired pluripotent cells. But few people have seen the implications of these developments for the cloning debate: Cloning for the purpose of biomedical research has lost its chief scientific raison d'etre. Reprogram-ming of adult cells provides personalized, rejection-proof stem cells, of known genetic make-up, directly from adults, and more efficiently than would cloning. No need for human eggs, no need to create and destroy cloned embryos, no need for the inefficient process of deriving stem cell colonies from cloned blastocysts. Ian Wilmut himself, the British scientist who cloned Dolly the sheep, has abandoned his research on cloning human embryos to work with reprogrammed adult cells.

Another effect of this breakthrough is that the value for stem cell research of the spare embryos that have accumulated in IVF [in vitro fertilization] clinics has diminished consider-ably, defusing the issue of the ban on federal funding of such research. Why work to derive new stem cell lines from frozen embryos (of unknown quality and unknown genetic composition, and with limited therapeutic potential owing to transplant immunity issues) when one can work with iPSCs to perfect the reprogramming approach and avoid all these difficulties?

A Triple-pronged Approach

That's not the only way the new scientific landscape changes the policy and legislative pictures. We are now able to disentangle and independently advance all three of the goods we care about. First, it now makes great sense to beef up federal support for regenerative medicine, prominently featuring ramped-up work with iPSCs (and other non-embryo-destroying sources of pluripotent human stem cells). The timing is perfect. The promise is great. The potential medical payoff is enormous. And the force of example for future public policy is clear: If we exercise both our scientific wit and our moral judgment, we can make biomedical progress, within moral boundaries, in ways that all citizens can happily support.

Second, we should call for a legislative ban on all attempts to conceive a child save by the union of egg and sperm (both taken from adults). This would ban human cloning to produce children, but also other egregious forms of baby making that would deny children a link to two biological parents, one male and one female, both adults. This approach differs from both the Kennedy-Feinstein-Hatch and the Brownback-Landrieu bills, yet it could—and should—gain support from people previously on both sides. It pointedly neither endorses nor restricts creating cloned embryos for research: Cloning embryos for research is no longer of such interest to scientists; therefore, it is also no longer, as a practical matter, so important to the pro-life cause. Moreover, the prohibited deed, operationally, should be the very act of creating the conceptus (with intent to transfer it to a woman for pregnancy), not, as the Kennedy-Feinstein-Hatch bill would have it, the transfer of the proscribed conceptus to the woman, a ban that would have made it a federal offense not to destroy the newly created cloned human embryos. The ban proposed here thus deserves the support of all, regardless of their position on embryo research.

Third, the time is also ripe for a separate bill to defend nascent life, by setting up a reasonable boundary in the realm of embryo research. We should call for a (four- or five-year) moratorium on all de novo creation—by whatever means—of human embryos for use in research. This would block the creation of embryos for research not only by cloning (or SCNT), the goal of the Brownback-Landrieu anti-cloning bill, but also by IVF. Such a prohibition can now be defended on practical as well as moral grounds. Many human embryonic stem cell lines exist and are being used in research; 21 such lines, still viable, are available for federally funded research, while an even greater number are being studied using private funds. The new iPSC research, however, suggests that our society can medically afford, at least for the time being, to put aside further creation of new human life merely to serve as a natural resource and research tool. We can now prudently shift the burden of proof to those who say such exploitative and destructive practices are absolutely necessary to seek cures for disease, and we can require more than vague promises and strident claims as grounds for overturning the moratorium.

Morally and strategically speaking, this triple-pronged approach has much to recommend it. It is at once more principled, more ambitious, and more likely to succeed than its predecessors. By addressing separately the cloning and embryo-research issues, we can fight each battle exactly on the principle involved: defense of human procreation or defense of human life. By broadening the first ban to include more than cloning, we can erect a barrier against all practices that would deny children born with the aid of reproductive technologies the ties enjoyed by children conceived naturally. By extending the second ban to cover all creation of life solely as an experimental tool, we can protect more than merely embryos created by cloning. We would force everyone to vote on the clear principles involved: Legislators would have to vote yea or nay on both weird forms of baby-making and the creation of human life solely for research, without bamboozling anyone with terminological sleights of hand. And by combining these legislative restrictions with strong funding initiatives for regenerative medicine, we can show the American people and the world that it is possible to vigorously pursue the cures all dearly want without sacrificing the humanity we rightly cherish.

Politically as well, this triple-pronged approach is a winner for all sides. Because the latest science has made creating embryos for research unnecessary and inefficient by comparison with reprogramming, we have the chance to put stem cell science on a footing that all citizens can endorse. Indeed, in return for accepting a moratorium on a scientific approach that is not very useful (creation of new embryos for research), scientists could exact large sums in public support for an exciting area of science. With pro-lifers as their biggest allies, they could obtain the research dollars they need—and their supposed enemies would write the biggest checks. Meanwhile, at the very time the latest science has made affronts to human procreation—cloning, but not only cloning—more likely and even imminent, pro-lifers and scientists can come together to ban these practices in America, as they have already been banned in the rest of the civilized world, without implicating the research debate at all.

In an election year, Congress will be little moved to act quickly on these seemingly low priority items. Moreover, the partisans who have produced the current impasse may still prefer to keep things at stalemate, the better to rally their constituents against the other side. But we can ill afford to be complacent. The science is moving very rapidly. Before the end of the summer [of 2008], we may well hear of the cloning of primate babies or perhaps even of a human child. Now is the time for action, before it is too late.

Periodical Bibliography

The following articles have been selected to supplement the diverse views presented in this chapter.

Adelle M. Banks	"Conscience Clauses Not Just About Abortion Anymore," *USA Today*, October 24, 2009.
Stuart Blackman	"Promises, Promises," *Scientist*, November 2009.
Stuart Farber	"At End of Life, Listen to Patient's Fears, Values," *American Medical News*, January 26, 2009.
James R. Harrigan	"Death Tourism," *FrontPage Magazine*, November 1, 2007.
Brandon Keim	"Designer Babies: A Right to Choose?" *Wired*, March 9, 2009.
William McGurn	"God vs. Science Isn't the Issue," *Wall Street Journal*, October 13, 2009.
Mike Pence	"The Empty Promise of Embryonic Stem Cell Research," *Christianity Today*, March 23, 2009.
Munier Salem	"Medicine and Money Do Not Mix," *Cornell University Daily Sun*, October 27, 2009.
Arthur Schafer	"The Great Canadian Euthanasia Debate," *Globe & Mail* (Toronto), November 5, 2009.
Rob Stein and Michelle Boorstein	"Vatican Ethics Guide Stirs Controversy," *Washington Post*, December 13, 2008.
John Tierney	"Are Scientists Playing God? It Depends on Your Religion," *New York Times*, November 20, 2007.

OPPOSING
VIEWPOINTS®
SERIES

CHAPTER 4

Are Ethics in Business Practices Beneficial?

Chapter Preface

In 2006, Bono of the rock band U2 and activist Bobby Shriver launched Product (RED) to raise money and awareness for the Global Fund to Fight AIDS, Tuberculosis, and Malaria. The brand has partnerships with major companies such as Apple, Converse, and The Gap, which sell (RED) MP3 players, limited-edition sneakers, and clothing and accessories, respectively. The Global Fund receives a portion of the profits of each item sold. In July 2009, the campaign claimed on its blog to have raised $130 million in three years, adding, "To date, the programs supported by (RED) and Global Fund financed grants have reached more than 4 million people."

Skeptics raise questions about Product (RED)'s combination of corporate enterprise and social activism, referred to as "cause marketing." Laura Starita, managing editor of *Philanthropy Action*, insists it will not be able to sustain profits. "More than anything," she says, "(RED) products are appealing to a sense of hip, an aesthetic which appeals to people who are by definition young and fickle." Furthermore, commentators argue that Product (RED) undermines genuine charity and individual responsibility. "First, it is self-serving, further diminishing true altruism in the corporate world," maintains Mark Rosenman, director of grant-making strategy group Caring to Change. "Second, all of us need to understand that, in the words of Buy(Less), shopping is not a solution. We cannot consume our way to charity and to a better world."

Other industry professionals defend the Product (RED) campaign. "Don't get me wrong, money's great, but cause marketing delivers so much more," contends Joe Waters, director of cause marketing at Boston Medical Center. "Look at the exposure (RED) has generated for the plight of AIDS victims in Africa. Look at how well known and respected (RED) has become as a charity in less than a year." Mike Swenson, president of Barkley Public Relations, agrees with Waters: "One thing he reminded me of is something I do believe strongly—any awareness, education, and money raised for any cause is a good thing." In the following chapter, the authors debate the ethical side of business practices.

"*Being an ethical, socially responsible company can attract investors, customers and top talent—and help ward off government regulators and environmental and labor activists.*"

Corporations Benefit from Ethical Practices

Adrienne Fox

In the following viewpoint, Adrienne Fox maintains that integrating ethical practices or a social cause into a company's agenda the right way can be socially responsible, productive, and profitable. Fox asserts that adopting a policy of corporate social responsibility (CSR) cannot be taken lightly, but can enhance a brand's relationship with consumers and draw top talent. In addition, she asserts that engaging employees in sustainability or other issues at the workplace can boost morale and efficiency. The author is a business writer and former managing editor of HR Magazine.

As you read, consider the following questions:

1. Why has the CSR movement increased, in Fox's view?

Adrienne Fox, "Corporate Social Responsibility Pays Off: By Being Good Corporate Citizens, Companies Can Woo Top Talent, Engage Employees and Raise Productivity," *HR Magazine*, vol. 52, August 2007, pp. 42–47. Copyright © Society for Human Resource Management 2007. Reproduced by permission.

2. What expectations are being placed on corporations, according to Bob Willard, as cited by the author?

3. As stated by Fox, how did jobseekers respond to Capgemini's socially responsible recruiting effort?

People who do charitable work often talk about how rewarding it is. Companies, too, have long been in the giving business for the same reason. But some organizations are finding that it's also financially rewarding to be socially responsible.

Call it the next generation of corporate philanthropy. Instead of simply writing checks to a charitable organization, companies are more closely integrating their cause agendas into their business strategies. It's called corporate social responsibility (CSR), also known as corporate sustainability or corporate citizenship. And it's paying off in many ways.

In today's post-Enron era[1], being an ethical, socially responsible company can attract investors, customers and top talent—and help ward off government regulators and environmental and labor activists.

Ben & Jerry's and The Body Shop pioneered the practice of marketing social responsibility as a business philosophy in the 1970s and 1980s. But the movement accelerated in recent years, spurred by the Sept. 11, 2001, terrorist attacks, corporate scandals and growing environmental concerns.

"Company stakeholders, which include employees, customers, shareholders and society at large, are placing greater expectations on corporations," says Bob Willard, author of *The Sustainability Advantage: Seven Business Case Benefits of a Triple Bottom Line* (2002) and former senior manager of leadership development at IBM Canada. "It's no longer enough to turn a good profit; you have to demonstrate that you didn't make that profit at the expense of employees, the environment or society."

---

1. Enron, in the early 2000s, was involved in a scandal that resulted in the corporation's bankruptcy and came to epitomize corporate excesses and unethical practices.

Companies recognize CSR's dividends. Log on to the web site of any Fortune 500 company and you will likely find a prominent link to its CSR efforts, with some even launching massive media campaigns promoting their socially responsible endeavors. Think Gap's Product (Red) campaign for AIDS medicine, Citgo's low-cost heating oil for the poor, and GE's [General Electric's] Ecomagination initiative to create clean technologies.

While HR [human resources] has engaged in corporate philanthropy as a way to demonstrate good values, HR executives also are using CSR to position their companies competitively in a tight labor market, to engage current employees and to raise productivity.

The Business Case

CSR cannot be sold to executives as an "HR pet project," advises Gayle Porter, SPHR, GPHR, associate professor of the School of Business at Rutgers University in Camden, N.J.

"Even if you are taking the idea to executives that in spirit agree with corporate social responsibility, you are still going to have to make the business case for it," says Porter, who is a member of the Society for Human Resource Management's (SHRM) Corporate Social Responsibility Special Expertise Panel. "After all, those executives have to answer to shareholders or whoever is above them. It has to have some relationship to the business."

Where social good overlaps with business opportunity is what Andy Savitz calls the "sweet spot." Savitz, a partner in the Sustainable Business Strategies consulting firm in Boston and author of *The Triple Bottom Line* (2006), points to Toyota's success with the hybrid car Prius as an example. It helps protect the environment while driving the carmaker to the No. 1 spot in the United States.

Another example is London-based Unilever's Project Shakti in India, which is training thousands of women in rural India to sell the company's personal hygiene products to the country's vast, untapped rural market.

"Consumer products companies are trying to understand how to do business with very poor people that will raise them out of poverty," says Savitz. "It's a perfect example of the sweet spot—creating markets where none now exist."

Before people get cynical about making money out of a social cause, experts argue that a company cannot pursue sustainable environmental and social initiatives without being sustainable economically.

"It's a three-legged stool of profits, people and the planet where without one leg the rest fail," says Willard.

It's the people leg that provides the most direct impact for HR involvement.

A 2007 SHRM corporate social responsibility survey of 431 U.S. HR professionals found that 91 percent said their company participated in CSR practices. The most common practices consisted of some sort of donations and volunteering.

But among more strategic CSR initiatives, fewer than half said they considered the overall social impact of their business decisions; 34 percent monitor the impact of business on the environment; and only a quarter align product or company marketing with a social cause.

"HR is just starting to awaken to the connections between what its role is in some of the sustainability issues," says Willard.

When HR recognizes the opportunity, there are quantifiable returns. Willard has identified seven business benefits for companies pursuing a sustainability strategy, three of which fall under HR—enhanced recruitment, higher retention of top talent and increased employee productivity.

"The power of sustainability for HR is that it incorporates what HR is already doing, but it integrates it with the business and with other key functions of the company and ties the whole package to strategy and the business case," says Savitz.

Once everything is packaged under CSR, HR can begin to leverage its efforts in related, but more strategic, ways, such as employment branding campaigns, employee engagement and enhanced productivity through environmentally friendly workspaces.

Employment Branding Through CSR

According to the 2003 CSR Monitor by GlobeScan, 70 percent of North American students surveyed said they would not apply for a job at a company deemed socially irresponsible. What's more, the survey found that 68 percent disagreed that salary was more important than social responsibility. A 2003 Stanford University study, Corporate Social Responsibility Reputation Effects on MBA Job Choice, found that MBA [master of business administration] graduates would sacrifice an average of $13,700 in salary to work for a socially responsible company.

Talent-strapped companies have found that CSR can be a draw in a crowded labor marketplace and can grab the attention of a certain type of highly skilled, highly motivated employee.

Take Capgemini in the Netherlands. [In 2006], the IT [information technology] consulting firm found itself facing the daunting challenge of filling 800 IT and management consulting positions in the Netherlands. "In all traditional markets, all of the recruiting-efforts we were doing were the same as our competitors," recalls Henk Wesselo, director of strategy and people relationship management.

Based on a suggestion from a company recruiter, Capgemini launched a market research tool to survey IT and management consultants on recruitment and retention factors.

Instead of going for the usual bait of awarding each respondent with a T-shirt or coffee mug for completion of the survey, Capgemini decided to fund a week of housing and schooling for poor children in India through a foundation in Kolkata [formerly known as Calcutta].

The survey then morphed into a recruiting tool by asking respondents to "opt in" if they wanted to learn more about opportunities at the company and to submit their resumes.

The response was overwhelming. Nearly 10,000 responded to the 30-minute survey. More than 2,000 people who submitted resumes fit the profile for Capgemini. Soon after, 800 candidates were interviewed, screened and hired. The remaining qualified candidates became part of a newly created Applicant Relationship Management project to keep in touch with until new positions open or are created.

Not only did Capgemini tie recruiting to CSR and fill 800 positions with what Wesselo says were top-quality candidates, but the company also received rich data to mine to tailor future recruiting efforts. In addition, media attention in the Netherlands for the campaign enhanced Capgemini's brand awareness among IT and management consultants as a socially responsible company.

The campaign also succeeded as an internal employee branding strategy as the company also donated two weeks of housing and schooling for the children in India for each employee referral who was hired during the campaign.

"We had a lot of direct impact but a lot of indirect impact as well," says Corporate Recruitment Manager Hein van Leeuwen, who ran the campaign. Most important, through its effort, Capgemini raised 10,400 weeks of housing and education for children in Kolkata.

Engaging Employees via CSR

Instead of just cutting a check to a foundation, companies find that the connection between CSR and employee engagement is deeper if employees are directly involved.

"After years in HR, I'm convinced that the only thing that motivates employees is employees themselves," says Willard. "One of the most powerful catalysts for that is the opportunity to contribute to society, to make a difference and do something that resonates with [employees'] values."

For an example, look no further than GE, which is currently reaping the fruits of this proposition from its multibillion-dollar Ecomagination initiative.

"The way we engage people in citizenship is living out three pillars of our citizenship philosophy: Make money; make it ethically; make a difference," says Bob Corcoran, vice president of corporate citizenship at GE in Fairfield, Conn.

Launched by CEO [chief executive officer] Jeffrey Immelt in 2005, Ecomagination seeks to enhance financial and environmental performance to drive company growth.

The initiative sets out an ambitious plan to invest in clean technology research and development, introduce "green" products for its customers, and reduce the company's own greenhouse gas emissions. Every aspect of the initiative is driven by innovation from its employees.

"We engage employees not just in the design phase of products that came out of Ecomagination, but we have Ecomagination contests to come up with ways to reduce energy—such as relamping factories, using solar panels or finding new routes for delivery trucks," Corcoran says. "The intent is to engage [employees] to find solutions."

Those solutions include energy-efficient appliances, compact fluorescent lighting and wind turbine power.

"Green is green," says Corcoran, quoting Immelt. "There's money to be made in the environment and in making the world green."

Indeed, GE is doubling its investment in green technologies from $750 million in 2004 to $1.5 billion in 2009. And it plans to double revenues from certified green technologies from $10 billion to $20 billion over the same period.

Heavy Responsibilities

Corporations—especially publicly quoted [publicly traded] corporations—do carry very heavy responsibilities. These responsibilities are not just defined by law. . . . They also cover many other areas where good corporate governance is coterminous with ensuring that the highest standards of corporate governance are achieved through a well-managed and monitored programme of CSR [corporate social responsibility]. What is different today is that corporation reputations are increasingly being assessed on these terms. Get it wrong and your reputation could be tarnished.

Richard Tudway,
Ethical Corporation, *February 5, 2002.*

"It's all about growth for the company," Corcoran says.

GE has developed an internal certification process called the Ecomagination Product Review scorecard that quantifies each product's environmental impacts and benefits relative to other products. The products are externally verified by an organization called GreenOrder.

Employee Solutions

A CSR initiative doesn't have to be a massive billion-dollar project such as GE's to inspire employees to make a positive impact on the environment while making the company money or cutting expenses. It can be as simple as recycling or reusing materials that would otherwise end up in a landfill, or retrofitting a building to make it more environmentally sound.

"At its most basic, HR can ask employees how they can help the company save money environmentally," says Willard.

"Turning off lights and computers at the end of the day is one example. But don't just pocket the money for the company. Share a percentage of the savings with employees. That's how you change the behaviors of employees."

To go even further, Savitz says HR should engage employees in environmental solutions through training and awareness and incentives.

One example of this is at Cascade Engineering, a plastics manufacturer based in Grand Rapids, Mich., with 1,100 employees. It provides employee training on what sustainability means and on how to participate in environmental solutions at the company.

"We have a number of employees with patents and encourage innovation," explains Kenyatta Brame, vice president of business services with responsibility for HR.

For example, the company developed a plastic BioSand water filter—to replace heavy concrete ones—that provides clean drinking water for people in developing countries. "It's very portable—about 8 pounds—and can provide fresh water for life for a family," says Fred Keller, founder and CEO of Cascade. Christian relief organization International Aid, based in Spring Lake, Mich., buys the filters and distributes them in Africa, raising money through individual and corporate donations and government and agency grants.

Cascade Engineering promotes employee involvement through an employee suggestion program. The basic philosophy is to involve all employees in small, daily improvements in their work areas.

For example, "an employee designed a cart system that had different compartments to put scrap items in," says Brame. "Employees looked at those items to see which items could be recycled back into the production process. We reduced our waste to landfills and our expenses by incorporating this into our manufacturing process." . . .

Spreading the CSR Message

To keep employees thinking about CSR solutions, more than two-thirds of U.S. companies with a formal CSR policy spread the word through company newsletters and other publications, according to the SHRM CSR survey. Only 9 percent produced a CSR annual report.

Cascade creates an annual CSR report and announces sustainability milestones companywide. "It's about understanding the problem and making a change," says Brame.

"The message of sustainability to individuals is quite powerful," adds CEO Keller. "We meet regularly and talk about what our [carbon] footprint is and ask what we can do to reduce our footprint. I haven't been to a meeting yet where people weren't excited about that."

Getting down to the individual level is important, says Brame. "Seeing sustainability day in and day out is hard. If you make the picture too big, people won't understand. If you take small aspects of it and relate it to people's jobs, and make them understand what they can do to effect change and make the company more sustainable, you can be successful."

> *"Private entities have ... , via the social responsibility notion, been converted into crypto-public enterprises that are the essence of socialism."*

Corporations Should Not Prioritize Ethical Practices

Henry G. Manne

In the following viewpoint, Henry G. Manne argues that the resources of private corporations should not be used for altruism and charity, including corporate social responsibility (CSR). He asserts that CSR confuses free enterprise with socialism, and when a corporation assumes a public interest, it is subject to state regulation or to acting as if it is owned by the public. As a result, the push for CSR transforms individuals' private investments into publicly used assets, he says. Mann is dean emeritus of the George Mason University School of Law.

As you read, consider the following questions:

1. What declaration is Milton Friedman famous for, as stated by the author?

2. How does Manne describe the origins of a corporation?

3. Who are proponents of CSR, in the author's view?

Milton Friedman [a noted economist] famously declared that the sole business of the managers of a publicly held corporation was to maximize the value of its outstanding shares. Any effort to use corporate resources for purely altruistic purposes he equated to socialism. He proposed that corporation law should prevent managers from straying off the reservation to join the altruists, a power now almost universally granted them by state legislation.

At a conference 34 years ago [in 1972], celebrating Friedman's 60th birthday, I presented a paper questioning that dictum by noting that the vast part of apparently nonprofit-oriented behavior by corporate managers was really—and necessarily—a profit-maximizing response to business, social or political pressures dressed up to look like something else. For such a strategy to be successful, the behavior had to appear to be nonprofit maximizing, and, of course, had to be called something like "social responsibility."

Since it was difficult or impossible to distinguish a profit motive from a charitable motive in any particular corporate action, a strong rule against corporate altruism, as Friedman was advocating, would invite judges to examine the propriety of a significant set of managerial decisions. I argued that American corporation law had traditionally had a strong "business judgment" rule whose principle aim was to prevent judges from even engaging in that kind of examination, which they were perhaps more likely to get wrong than to get right. Thus, if any plausible basis existed for a bona fide managerial decision, no matter how charitable it looked, I argued, we did not want a stronger rule that would invite judges to second guess managers.

The assembled audience of Friedmanites, as we were sometimes called—*Are we all Friedmanites now?*—was aghast that I dared to counter one of the master's most pointed proposals, and the immediate response from the audience was hostile. Well, it was, until Friedman took the floor to declare that "I agree with everything that Henry said." That settled that. I assumed that I would not hear Friedman again declaring that corporate social responsibility was the equivalent of socialism. Consequently, I was chagrined over the ensuing years to hear him make the same pronouncement many times, though to my knowledge not with any explicit proposal for a change in the legal rule.

Private to Public Responsibility

Now I realize (I should have known) he was absolutely correct about the significance of proposals for socially responsible corporate behavior, whether they emanated from within or outside the corporation. These proposals reflect, as well as anything else happening today, the inability of many commentators to distinguish between private and public property—in other words, between a free enterprise system and socialism. Somehow large-scale business success, usually resulting in a publicly held company, seems mysteriously to transform the nature of numerous individuals' private investments into assets affected with a public interest. And once these corporate behemoths are "affected with a public interest," they must either be regulated by the state or they must act as though they are owned by the public, and are therefore inferentially a part of the state. This attitude is reflected not merely by corporate activists, but by many "modern" corporate managers.

An integral part of the older notion of public utility regulation required that the enterprise be, or act like, a monopoly (whether "natural" or not), in order to be affected with a public interest. But in today's confusion, there is no such requirement. No arguments, weak as they are, about natural monopoly, market failure, government creation of corporations or the alleged government gifts of limited liability and per-

A Niche Market

Part of the reason why CSR does not necessarily pay is that only a handful of consumers know or care about the environmental or social records of more than a handful of firms. "Ethical" products are a niche market: Virtually all goods and services continue to be purchased on the basis of price, convenience and quality.

David Vogel,
Forbes, *October 16, 2008.*

petual existence, are required to justify the demands now regularly placed on business entities. Any large enterprise, no matter how competitive its industry and no matter how successfully it is fulfilling the public's desires, has a social responsibility—a term that makes mockery of the idea of individual responsibility—to use part of its resources for "public" endeavors. Today's favorite causes are environmental protection, employee health, sales of goods at below-market prices, weather modification, community development, private enforcement of (not merely abiding by) government regulations and support of cultural, educational and medical facilities.

How did this transposition from private to public responsibility come about? After all, even the largest corporation started simply as an idea in someone's head. At first this person hires employees, borrows capital or sells equity, produces goods or service and markets a product. Nothing about any of these purely private and benign arrangements suggests a public interest in the outcome. But then the business begins to grow, family stock holdings become more diffused, additional capital is required and, *voilà*, another publicly held corporation. In other words, another American success story.

But what has happened to implicate public involvement in the management or governance of these enterprises as they grew from a mere idea? Nothing. And if that nothing be multiplied by tens or hundreds or thousands, the product is still zero. So where along the line to enormous size and financial heft has the public-private nexus necessarily changed? True, there are now a large number of complex and specialized private contracts, but every single one of these transactions is based on private property, freedom of contract, and individual risk and reward. If one apple is a fruit, even a billion apples do not become meat.

The origins of this transformation lie in the minds of people who do not like or appreciate the genius of capitalist success stories, including always politicians, who will generally make any argument in order to control more private wealth. Of course, the social responsibility of corporations is always tied to the proponents' own views of compassion or justice or avoidance of a cataclysm. But the logic of their own arguments requires that essentially private corporations be viewed as somehow "public" in nature. That is, the public, or the preferred part of it, often termed "stakeholders" (another shameful semantic play, this time on the word "shareholders"), has a pseudo-ownership interest in every large corporation. Without that dimension in their argument, free market logic would prevail.

The Essence of Socialism

The illusion of great and threatening power, the superficial attractiveness of the notion, and the frequent repetition of the mantra of corporate social responsibility have made this fallacy a part of the modern corporate zeitgeist. Like the citizens who were afraid to tell the emperor that he was naked, no responsible business official would dare contradict the notion publicly for fear of financial ruin, even though the practice continues to cost shareholders and society enormous amounts.

This is especially so in large-scale retail businesses like Wal-Mart or Coca-Cola or BP [British Petroleum] that are highly vulnerable to organized public criticism. Our laws against extortion do not function effectively when it comes to corporations. And so to some extent these private entities have indeed, via the social responsibility notion, been converted into crypto-public enterprises that are the essence of socialism. Milton Friedman was right again.

| *"What might be called the 'ethical subprime lending' industry . . . sport[s] healthy payback rates."*

Subprime Lending Is Ethical Because It Can Benefit Americans

Daniel Gross

Daniel Gross is a senior editor at Newsweek, *where he writes the Contrary Indicator column. In the following viewpoint, Gross maintains that not all subprime lending—the most risky type of loan—is exploitative. On the contrary, the author contends that ethical, community-oriented lenders give opportunities to many first-time, working-class Americans to buy homes or obtain loans. These lenders carefully assess applications, do not persuade customers to take high-interest loans, and hold on to loans rather than resell them, Gross says. As a result, Gross maintains that the foreclosure and delinquency rates are far less than the national average for subprime loans.*

As you read, consider the following questions:

1. What organizations do community development financial institutions (CDFI) include, according to the author?

2. How does Shorebank help its customers keep up with mortgages, as described by Gross?

3. How has the mortgage crisis affected ethical subprime lending, in the author's view?

In recent months, conservative economists and editorialists have tried to pin the blame for the unholy international financial mess on subprime lending and subprime borrowers. If bureaucrats and social activists hadn't pressured firms to lend to the working poor, the narrative goes, we'd still be partying like it was 2005 and [collapsed investment bank and brokerage firm] Bear Stearns would be a going concern. The *Wall Street Journal's* editorial page has repeatedly heaped blame on the Community Reinvestment Act (CRA), the 1977 law aimed at preventing redlining in minority neighborhoods. Fox Business Network anchor Neil Cavuto in September [2008] proclaimed that "loaning to minorities and risky folks is a disaster."

This line of reasoning is absurd on several levels. Many of the biggest subprime lenders weren't banks, and thus weren't covered by the CRA. Nobody forced Bear Stearns to borrow $33 for every dollar of assets it had, and [government-run mortgage companies] Fannie Mae and Freddie Mac didn't coerce highly compensated CEOs [chief executive officers] into rolling out no-money-down, exploding adjustable-rate mortgages. Banks will lose just as much money lending to really rich white guys like former Lehman Brothers CEO Richard Fuld as they will on loans to poor people of color in the South Bronx.

But the best refutation may be provided by Douglas Bystry, president and CEO of Clearinghouse CDFI (community development financial institution), based in Lake Forest, Calif. Since 2003, this for-profit firm in Orange County—home to busted subprime behemoths like Ameriquest—has made $220 million in mortgages in the Golden State's subprime killing fields. More than 90 percent of its home loans have gone to first-time buyers, about half of whom are minorities. Out of 770 single-family loans it has made, how many foreclosures have there been? "As far as we know," says Bystry, "seven." [In 2007] Clearinghouse reported a $1.4 million pretax profit.

The Ethical Lending Industry

Community-development banks, credit unions and other CDFIs—a mixture of faith-based and secular, for-profit and not-for-profit organizations—constitute what might be called the "ethical subprime lending" industry. Even amid the worst housing crisis since the 1930s, many of these institutions sport healthy payback rates. They haven't bankrupted their customers or their shareholders. Nor have they rushed to Washington begging for bailouts. Their numbers include tiny startups and veterans like Chicago's ShoreBank, founded in 1973, which now sports $2.3 billion in assets, 418 employees and branches in Detroit and Cleveland. Cliff Rosenthal, CEO of the National Federation of Community Development Credit Unions, notes that for his organization's 200 members, which serve predominantly low-income communities, "delinquent loans are about 3.1 percent of assets." In the second quarter, by contrast, the national delinquency rate on subprime loans was 18.7 percent.

Participants in this "opportunity finance" field, as it is called, aren't a bunch of squishy social workers. In order to keep their doors open, they have to charge appropriate rates—slightly higher than those on prime, conforming loans—and manage risk properly. They judge their results on financial performance and on the impact they have on the communities they serve. "We have to be profitable, just not profit-maximizing," says Mark Pinsky, president and CEO of the Opportunity Finance Network, an umbrella group for CDFIs that in 2007 collectively lent $2.1 billion, with charge-offs of less than 0.75 percent.

What sets the "good" subprime lenders apart is that they never bought into all the perverse incentives and "innovations" of the late subprime lending system—the fees paid to mortgage brokers, fancy offices and the reliance on securitization. Like a bunch of present-day George Baileys [fictional character from the movie *It's a Wonderful Life*], ethical subprime lenders evaluate applications carefully, don't pay brokers big fees to rope customers into high-interest loans and mostly hold onto the loans they make rather than reselling them. They focus less on quantity than on quality. Clearinghouse's borrowers must qualify for the fixed-rate mortgages they take out. "If one of our employees pushed someone into a house they couldn't afford, they would be fired," says CEO Bystry.

These lenders put into practice the types of bromides that financial-services companies like to use in their advertising. "We're in business to improve people's lives and do asset building," says Linda Levy, CEO of the Lower East Side Credit Union. The 7,500-member nonprofit, based on still-scruffy Avenue B, doesn't serve the gentrified part of Manhattan's Lower East Side, with its precious boutiques and million-dollar lofts. The average balance in its savings accounts is $1,400. The typical member? "A Hispanic woman from either Puerto Rico or the Dominican Republic in her late 40s or early 50s, on government assistance, with a bunch of kids," Levy says. Sure sounds like subprime. But the delinquency rate on its portfolio of mortgage and consumer loans is 2.3 percent, and it's never had a foreclosure.

Compensating Lenders

Compared with conventional mortgages, the subprime variety typically involved higher interest rates and stiff prepayment penalties.

To many critics, these features were proof of evil intent among lenders. But the higher rates compensated lenders for higher default rates. And the prepayment penalties made sure that people whose credit improved couldn't just refinance somewhere else at a lower rate, thus leaving the lenders stuck with the rest, including those whose credit had worsened.

Robert J. Shiller, New York Times, *July 19, 2009.*

Ethical subprime lenders have to look beyond credit scores and algorithms when making lending judgments. Homewise, based in Santa Fe, N.M., which lends to first-time, working-class home buyers, makes credit decisions based in part on whether borrowers have scraped together a 2 percent down payment. "If customers build a savings habit to save that money on a modest income, it says a lot about them and their financial discipline," says executive director Mike Loftin. Of the 500 loans on Homewise's books in September [2005], only 0.6 percent were 90 days late. That compares with 2.35 percent of all prime mortgages nationwide.

Since ethical subprime lenders know they're going to live with the loans they make—rather than simply sell them—they invest in initiatives that will make it more likely the loans will be paid back. Faith Community United Credit Union, which got started in the basement of a Baptist church in Cleveland in 1952 with members saving quarters on Sundays, now has $10 million in assets. In addition to making loans, "we teach people how to manage their finances and accounts," says CEO Rita Haynes. ShoreBank, as part of its energy-conservation loan program, offers free energy audits and a free Energy Star refrigerator when upgrades are completed. The theory: reducing energy bills makes it more likely people will stay current with their mortgages. Today, only $4.83 million of ShoreBank's $1.5 billion loans are in foreclosure, or just 0.32 percent.

Beyond Mortgages

Ethical subprime lenders are now expanding beyond mortgages. Ed Jacob, manager and CEO of Chicago's North Side Community Federal Credit Union, was alarmed to learn that many of his 2,700 members, most of whom have less than $100 in their accounts, were relying on the "second-tier financial-service marketplace": check-cashing outlets and payday lenders, which charge exorbitant fees. So he rolled out a Payday Alternative Loan (PAL), $500 for six months at 16.5 percent. The delinquency rate on the more than 5,000 PALs extended thus far is 2.5 percent. "For payday lenders, it's a success if customers keep taking out loans. To me, it's a success if they don't have to anymore," Jacob says. He believes such loans can build a credit history and help "move people to better products for them and us—auto loans and, eventually, mortgage loans."

Lending small amounts of money, carefully and responsibly, to working-class people isn't a recipe for riches or grand executive living. At the headquarters of ShoreBank, which occupies a former movie theater built in 1923, the window in one founder's office looks out onto a brick wall. Bystry, the CEO of Clearinghouse CDFI, earns a salary of $190,000, a pittance compared with the compensation of larger lenders. (Angelo Mozilo, former CEO of Countrywide Financial, was paid $22.1 million in 2007.) For all the growth, this remains very much a niche industry.

Still, the mortgage crisis has provided an opportunity for ethical subprime lenders to expand. ShoreBank has added staffers and in August 2007 rolled out a Rescue Loan program, which aims to move borrowers out of expensive adjustable-rate mortgages into fixed-rate loans. "We really believe we can help people caught in these bad mortgages," says Jean Pogge, executive vice president of consumer and community banking at ShoreBank. And with plenty of lenders having failed or pulled back from markets, new customers are flocking to their doors. "We're getting demand for regular co-op loans for the first time," says Levy of the Lower East Side Credit Union. In California, the news on housing may be unrelentingly grim, but through the third quarter, Clearinghouse CDFI made 161 loans for $48.4 million, up about 50 percent from the total in the first three quarters of 2007. Doug Bystry says, "This may be a record year for us."

| "Predatory lenders put borrowers into loans that they cannot afford."

Subprime Lending Is Unethical Because It Harms Americans

Alexander Gourse

In the following viewpoint, Alexander Gourse argues that unethical subprime lenders prey on the poor and minorities. Despite claims that these loans expand home ownership, Gourse claims that most are used to pay off consumer or personal debt. Moreover, subprime lenders use "bait-and-switch" tactics to deceive customers into taking out loans at the highest interest rates and maximum amounts, Gourse contends. Therefore, he maintains that funds for community development financial institutions (CDFI), which assist low-income borrowers with mortgage and loans, should be increased. The author is a doctoral student in U.S. history at Northwestern University.

As you read, consider the following questions:

1. How were Betty and Tyrone Walker tricked into accepting a high-interest loan, as stated by Gourse?

Alexander Gourse, "The Subprime Bait and Switch," *In These Times*, July 16, 2007. Reproduced by permission of the publisher, www.inthesetimes.com.

2. Why are low-income and minority borrowers subject to predatory lending, in the author's opinion?

3. How does Gourse compare white borrowers to black and Latino borrowers?

When the housing market began its rapid ascent in the mid-'90s, many observers waxed rhapsodic about the potential of high-interest, subprime loans to merge the financial interests of investors and low income and minority communities. The hope for subprime boosters was that such loans would allow the mortgage industry to continue business as usual while at the same time meeting government mandates for fair and affordable housing. As recently as April 2005, [former chairman of the Federal Reserve] Alan Greenspan praised the deregulation of the banking and lending industries for having "vastly expanded credit availability to virtually all income classes."

It's true that the number of minority homeowners increased at a similar rate to that of all homeowners during the last decade, but the housing market's recent [2007] slump has brought to light serious weaknesses in the subprime model, raising doubts about its viability as a tool for community reinvestment. The *Wall Street Journal* recently reported that Greenspan's zeal for deregulation may have caused him to turn a blind eye to predatory practices within the subprime lending industry, and consumer advocates are now predicting that nearly 20 percent of subprime mortgage loans made since 2005 will end in foreclosure, at a loss to the consumer of around $164 billion.

Risks and Rewards

The home mortgage industry divides would-be borrowers into two basic types. Prime borrowers are those who have adequate income and good credit histories. Subprime borrowers are those with problematic credit histories and, often, less-than-adequate incomes. The loans are inherently risky for the lender, as such borrowers are more likely to default on payments, requiring higher interest rates to offset this risk.

Before the mid-'90s, subprime lenders operated on a limited scale, but the rapid growth in the housing market brought with it more mortgage companies that specialized in subprime lending. The subprime industry grew from a $35 billion per year industry in 1994 to more than $330 billion in 2003, and from 2004 to 2006 the volume of subprime loans nearly doubled to more than $600 billion.

"These loans keep being made because investors make a profit," says Geoff Smith, research director at the Woodstock Institute, a Chicago-based nonprofit that specializes in issues of community economic development. "Investors can tolerate a certain number of losses, because failures are priced into the risk assessment. As long as investors are still profiting, mortgage companies will do whatever they can to make more loans, and to maximize the total sums loaned out."

While industry representatives have lauded their own success in offering credit to financially underserved populations, recent studies suggest that subprime loans have only a marginal effect on homeownership rates. Original purchase loans comprise only a small portion of subprime mortgages, and an even smaller percentage—about 9 percent—go to first-time homebuyers. A majority of subprime loans are refinances, with homeowners looking to lower their monthly payments or to draw out the equity in their homes to pay off their consumer debt or other personal expenses. If foreclosure rates continue to rise as predicted, the Center for Responsible Lending estimates that though some people will become first time homeowners due to subprime loans, there will be significantly more borrowers that will lose their homes to foreclosure.

The Subprime Bait and Switch

Industry representatives typically cite the poor credit histories of most subprime borrowers to explain increasing foreclosure rates. Consumer and community advocates, however, paint a darker picture. "Predatory lending is definitely a systemic problem within the subprime mortgage industry," says Al Hofeld Jr., a litigation attorney and chair of the South Side Community Federal Credit Union in Chicago (SSCFU). "There are very few subprime lenders who will make a subprime loan where the interest rate actually reflects the risk involved."

According to Smith, predatory lenders put borrowers into loans that they cannot afford. While blatant fraud, such as the falsification of a borrower's income to justify a larger loan, is becoming less common, the misrepresentation of a loan's characteristics, like the concealment of a fixed rate "teaser" period that adjusts upward after two years, is a growing problem.

Hofeld says subprime mortgage companies routinely use bait-and-switch tactics to lure in potential borrowers and maximize the amount of money loaned out. At closing, borrowers are often presented with terms that do not match those previously offered by the company, and then pressured into signing documents which they have not had time to review. Ameriquest Mortgage Company is currently facing hundreds of lawsuits which allege that they routinely baited potential customers by promising fixed interest rates, low or no fees, lower monthly payments, no prepayment penalties, or by representing to borrowers that they qualify for a particular set of terms.

In 2005, Betty and Tyrone Walker, a couple living in the Park Manor neighborhood on the south side of Chicago, took out a refinance loan with Ameriquest. "All we wanted to do was to make our house more livable," says Walker, who is legally disabled and is raising a 12-year-old adopted daughter on her husband's salary as a mail clerk at a local medical school. After being solicited by Ameriquest through the mail, the Walkers decided to use some of the equity in their home to refurnish their basement.

The Walkers requested information about the loan numerous times, and were confident that they knew what the terms of the loan would be when they went to sign the closing documents. "We just kept asking them whether we were going to remain on a fixed rate, and they just kept lying to us, telling us we'd get a fixed rate," Mrs. Walker alleges in a lawsuit against Ameriquest.

As they later discovered, however, the terms of the loan were not as they expected. Not only did the loan have an adjustable rate that can go as high as 13.4 percent, but the Walkers allege that Ameriquest falsely told them that their home had doubled in value since they had bought it a few years earlier, thus qualifying them for a larger loan amount. Ameriquest didn't give them copies of their loan documents at closing, and as a result the Walkers did not realize that the terms had been changed until well after the three-day period during which they could legally cancel the loan. They have since tried to refinance, but have been unable to find another lender willing to lend them the amount currently owed to Ameriquest; the artificially inflated appraisal value has in effect trapped them in a loan with a rising interest rate.

"I felt so stupid after I realized that I had been taken advantage of," says Walker. "I made them a lunch! I'm always cooking, so I offered them food. I thought they were doing such a swell job of helping us that I cooked for these people, oh lord."

The Race Factor

The Walkers' story is all too familiar. Predatory lending is a particularly widespread problem in low-income and minority communities, where a complex history of housing discrimination, racial segregation and a lack of access to affordable credit have left borrowers with few options. Though redlining, blockbusting and other discriminatory practices were banned in stages between 1968 and 1977, most banks are reluctant to open branches in black neighborhoods, a vacuum that is filled by currency exchanges, payday lenders and now subprime mortgage companies.

"Subprime lenders," says Smith, "are taking advantage of the fact that they're the only game in town." Individual brokers and loan officers make money by taking "points"—that is, charging percentage points of the loan amount, which are added to the borrower's closing costs—giving them an incentive to maximize the loan amount, regardless of the borrower's ability to pay for it.

According to "Paying More for the American Dream," a joint report from six national housing policy organizations, in 2005, black borrowers were 3.8 times more likely than whites to be placed in a high cost loan, while Hispanic borrowers were 3.6 times more likely than whites to receive such a loan. Income disparities between white and minority communities account for some of this difference, but Smith says the disparity is too large to be accounted for by income alone. Low-income black borrowers in the Chicago area were four times as likely to be put in high cost loans than low-income white borrowers.

But the largest disparity was in the highest income bracket, where blacks were five times as likely as whites to be placed in a high cost loan. Foreclosure rates in heavily minority neighborhoods across the nation follow these trends, with black and Latino neighborhoods experiencing significantly higher foreclosure rates than their white counterparts.

Regulation and Alternatives

Consumer fraud laws, including requirements that lenders disclose the terms of a loan and borrowers' cancellation rights, have been important tools for attorneys fighting predatory lenders. But with thousands of lawsuits filed on behalf of subprime borrowers across the country, many consumer advocates are calling for government regulation of the subprime industry.

No Justification

According to subprime lenders, the justification for the high cost of subprime lending is the increased risk associated with the low credit scores of subprime borrowers. However, there is evidence that approximately 50 percent of those borrowing in the subprime market would qualify for a prime loan. The practice of guiding credit-worthy borrowers into more expensive subprime loans is estimated to cost American consumers $9.1 billion a year.

Jeff R. Crump,
Implications, *August 2008.*

"Ideally, what we need is a federal law to make sure lenders are using appropriate qualifying standards so that borrowers can repay the loans," says Smith. Groups like the Center for Responsible Lending have also supported a ban on prepayment penalties and a reform of the "perverse compensation incentives" for "hazardous" loan products.

Congress however is unlikely to pass comprehensive legislation that deals with predatory lending, says Smith. "Realistically, we should be focusing on the state laws currently under debate." In 1999, North Carolina was the first state to regulate predatory lending practices and dozens of other states and municipalities have followed suit. This year alone [2007] legislation dealing with subprime and predatory lending has been introduced in 26 states.

Hofeld, however, sees regulation as only a partial solution. "Some of the laws regulating predatory lenders could be improved, but some of the problems we see are very difficult to regulate. You can't control what salespeople tell prospective borrowers."

What's more, warnings from the mortgage industry that regulation will cut off credit to low income and minority neighborhoods have created a panic among some community leaders and politicians. In Illinois, a bill mandating credit counseling for borrowers in several Chicago zip codes was suspended due to fears that it was racist and would slow real estate sales in those areas.

The seemingly no-win choice between disinvestment in low-income communities or allowing predatory lenders to operate freely might not be as bleak as it appears. A network of Community Development Financial Institutions (CDFIs) has emerged in some cities, providing affordable financial services to low-income individuals who might otherwise be prime targets for predatory lenders. Although their resources are limited, such institutions offer an alternative model for low-income community development.

"Our biggest problem is one of scale," Hofeld says about the SSCFU. "We want to get to the point where we have a large enough number of deposits so that we're making enough loans to be self sufficient."

With around 1,800 members and $3 million in assets, the SSCFU serves 33 neighborhoods on the south side of Chicago with a population of approximately 854,000 people. A self-described "financial institution with a social mission," the SSCFU is one of approximately 225 members of the National Federation of Community Development Credit Unions, a national organization working to establish a financial infrastructure in poor communities and empower low-income people through asset development.

While much of the capital required to operate the SSCFU has come from foundations and member deposits, federal money has been important as well. Established in 1994, the CDFI Fund within the Treasury Department has made resources available for community development to credit unions, banks and microenterprise funds.

"The CDFI Fund really is the single largest source of funding for these institutions," says Cliff Rosenthal, the executive director for the National Federation of Community Development Credit Unions. "Though they can grow slowly on their own, the Fund is the only source of major investment that allows these institutions to make quantum leaps in their work."

Since the [George W.] Bush administration took office [in 2001], however, the CDFI Fund has decreased by more than 50 percent. As a result, not only is funding harder to come by, but the maximum grants awarded by the Fund have decreased from around $3 million to $585,000.

Despite the lack of resources, community development credit unions like the SSFCU are proving that the usurious practices of predatory lenders are not a necessary evil in the fight for fair and affordable housing.

"The problems in the subprime mortgage industry should be framed as an affordable housing issue," says Hofeld. "We often compartmentalize the way we think about issues, but I really think that predatory lending is something that is decreasing the supply of affordable housing. And the lack of access to mortgage credit on fair terms is something that prevents people from getting into homes."

Periodical Bibliography

The following articles have been selected to supplement the diverse views presented in this chapter.

Lee Blum — "In Defense of Subprime," *Cornell University Daily Sun*, September 1, 2008.

Jon Entine — "Wal-Mart: Ethical Retailing—from Evil Empire to Jolly Green Giant," *Ethical Corporation*, July 4, 2008.

Alyssa Katz — "Predatory Lending with a Smiley Face," *Salon*, March 4, 2009. www.salon.com.

Paul Kirklin — "The Ultimate Pro-WalMart Article," *Mises Daily*, June 28, 2006.

Karen E. Klein — "Making the Case for Business Ethics," *BusinessWeek*, December 30, 2008.

Knowledge@Wharton — "In the Game of Business, Playing Fair Can Actually Lead to Greater Profits," March 13, 2008. www.knowledge.wharton.upenn.edu.

Gerald H. Lander, Katherine Barker, Margarita Zabelina, and Tiffany A. Williams — "Subprime Mortgage Tremors: An International Issue," *Entrepreneur*, February 2009.

Barry C. Lynn — "The Case for Breaking Up Wal-Mart," *Harper's*, July 24, 2006.

Bill McKibben — "Hype vs. Hope," *Mother Jones*, October 2006.

Michael C. Moynihan — "Big Box Panic," *Reason*, January 2008.

Michael Noer, David M. Ewalt, and Tara Weiss — "Corporate Social Responsibility," *Forbes*, October 16, 2008.

For Further Discussion

Chapter One

1. Do you agree or disagree with Jonathan Gilligan that today's society is responsible for the well-being of future generations? Why or why not?

2. Kenneth Boa maintains that Christian values are evident across religions. Do you agree or disagree with Boa's claim? Cite examples from the texts to support your response.

3. James Leroy Wilson, Karen Stephens, and Women & the Economy offer different reasons why people should behave ethically. In your opinion, who presents the most persuasive argument? Use examples from the viewpoints to explain your answer.

Chapter Two

1. David Koepsell asserts that Christians subjectively choose commandments to follow. What is your opinion on this? In your opinion, is Dennis Prager's case for Christian values based on subjective judgments? Why or why not? Use examples from the viewpoints to support your response.

2. Jack Russell Weinstein states that most discussions about moral education support the indoctrination of students with Christian beliefs. Do you agree or disagree with the author? Why or why not?

Chapter Three

1. Rosemary Tong insists that the use of embryos in science and medicine is similar to the donation of human bodies, organs, and tissues for research. Do you agree or disagree with the author? Use examples from the viewpoints to explain your answer.

2. Peter C. Glover contends that legalizing physician-assisted suicide would lead to involuntary euthanasia. Does Timothy E. Quill effectively counter this allegation? Explain, citing examples from the texts to support your response.

3. Leon R. Kass maintains that reproductive human cloning would result in the "manufacturing" of babies. Would Jacob M. Appel's arguments for reproductive human cloning lead to this scenario? Why or why not?

Chapter Four

1. Henry G. Manne argues that proponents of corporate social responsibility (CSR) have a negative opinion of capitalism. Would you characterize Adrienne Fox's position for CSR as anticapitalist? Explain your answer.

2. Daniel Gross and Alexander Gourse share a positive view of ethical, community-minded lending. Does this undermine Gourse's view against subprime loans? Use examples from the viewpoints to craft your response.

Organizations to Contact

The editors have compiled the following list of organizations concerned with the issues debated in this book. The descriptions are derived from materials provided by the organizations. All have publications or information available for interested readers. The list was compiled on the date of publication of the present volume; the information provided here may change. Be aware that many organizations take several weeks or longer to respond to inquiries, so allow as much time as possible.

American Medical Association (AMA)
515 N. State Street, Chicago, IL   60654
(800) 621-8335
Web site: www.ama-assn.org

The AMA is the largest professional association for medical doctors. It helps set standards for medical education and practices, and it is a powerful lobby in Washington for physicians' interests. Its ethics division specializes in issues concerning medical ethics. The association publishes a number of medical journals, as well as *American Medical News* and its flagship journal *JAMA*, both weeklies.

American Society of Law, Medicine, and Ethics (ASLME)
765 Commonwealth Ave., Suite 1634, Boston, MA   02215
(617) 262-4990 • fax: (617) 437-7596
e-mail: info@aslme.org
Web site: www.aslme.org

The society's members include physicians, attorneys, health care administrators, and others interested in the relationship between law, medicine, and ethics. ASLME takes no positions but acts as a forum for discussion of issues such as genetic engineering. The organization maintains an information clearinghouse and a library. Its publications include the *American Journal of Law & Medicine* and the *Journal of Law, Medicine, & Ethics*.

Canadian Bioethics Society
Lydia Riddell, 561 Rocky Ridge Bay NW
Calgary, AB   T3G 4E7
  CANADA
(403) 208-8027
e-mail: lmriddell@shaw.ca
Web site: www.bioethics.ca

The society's membership consists of physicians, nurses, health care administrators, lawyers, theologians, philosophers, and others concerned with the ethical and humane dimensions of health care. It seeks to provide a forum for the exchange of views and ideas concerning bioethics, as well as assistance with the practical problems of decisions at the clinical, professional, and policy levels. The society publishes a biannual newsletter.

Center for Applied Christian Ethics (CACE)
Wheaton College, Wheaton, IL   60187-5593
(630) 752-5886 • fax: (630) 752-5731
e-mail: cace@wheaton.edu
Web site: www.wheaton.edu/cace

CACE's goal is to raise moral awareness and elicit moral thinking by encouraging the application of Christian ethics to public policy and personal practice. The center sponsors conferences, workshops, and public debates on ethical issues. It produces a variety of resource materials, including audio downloads of lectures and the *CACE eJournal*.

Center for Applied and Professional Ethics (CAPE)
801 McClung Tower, University of Tennessee
Knoxville, TN   37996-0480
(865) 974-7210 • fax: (865) 974-3509
e-mail: dreidy@utk.edu

CAPE is concerned with the practical application of ethics in such areas as business, medicine, law, and the environment. The center holds biennial conferences on professional ethics, conducts research projects, performs community outreach, and maintains a resource center of publications and articles on applied ethics.

Center for Bioethics and Human Dignity (CBHD)

2065 Half Day Road, Deerfield, IL   60015
(847) 317-8180 • fax: (847) 317-8101
e-mail: info@cbhd.org
Web site: www.cbhd.org

The center's mission is to bring Christian perspectives to bear on contemporary bioethical challenges facing individuals, families, communities, and society. It sponsors projects and conferences on such topics as euthanasia, genetic technology, and abortion. In addition, CBHD offers case studies and bio-ethics podcasts.

Center for Business Ethics (CBE)

Bentley University, Waltham, MA   02452-4705
(781) 891-2981 • fax: (781) 891-2988
e-mail: cbeinfo@bentley.edu
Web site: www.bentley.edu/cbe

CBE is dedicated to promoting ethical business conduct in contemporary society. It helps corporations and other organizations strengthen their ethical cultures through educational programming and consulting. The center maintains a multimedia library, which contains one of the largest collections of business ethics books, journals, videos, and corporate ethics materials in the United States.

Center for Ethics and Human Rights

American Nurses Association (ANA)
Silver Spring, MD   20910-3492
(301) 628-5000 • fax: (301) 628-5001
e-mail: ethics@ana.org
Web site: www.nursingworld.org/ethics

The center is part of the ANA, a professional organization for nurses. It is committed to addressing the complex ethical issues confronting nurses and to increasing nurses' ethical competence and sensitivity to human rights. In addition, the center advocates public policies that address ethical issues in health care. It publishes the *Online Journal of Issues in Nursing (OJIN)*.

Common Cause

1133 Nineteenth Street NW, 9th Fl., Washington, DC   20036
(202) 833-1200
Web site: www.commoncause.org

Common Cause is a liberal lobbying organization that works to improve the ethical standards of Congress and government in general. Its priorities include campaign reform, making government officials accountable for their actions, and promoting civil rights for all citizens. The organization publishes position papers, reports, and a monthly newsletter.

EthicsCentre CA

One Yonge Street, Suite 1801, Toronto, ON   M5E 1W7
   CANADA
(416) 368-7525 • fax: (416) 369-0515
e-mail: hmyj@ethicscentre.ca
Web site: www.ethicscentre.ca

The centre includes corporations and individuals dedicated to developing and maintaining an ethical corporate culture. It supports research into issues concerning corporate ethics and sponsors seminars, conferences, and lectures on business ethics. It publishes the newsletter *Management Ethics*.

Ethics Resource Center

2345 Crystal Drive, Suite 201, Arlington, VA   22202
(703) 647-2185 • fax: (703) 647-2180
e-mail: ethics@ethics.org
Web site: www.ethics.org

The center works to restore America's ethical foundations by fostering integrity, ethical conduct, and basic values in the nation's institutions. It also strives to create international coalitions dedicated to global ethics. The center supports character education and has developed several video-based learning programs for use in schools. Its resources include publications, videos, subscriptions, educational tools, and the electronic newsletter *Ethics Today*.

Hastings Center

21 Malcolm Gordon Road, Garrison, NY   10524-4125
(845) 424-4040 • fax: (845) 424-4545
e-mail: mail@thehastingscenter.org
Web site: www.thehastingscenter.org

Since its founding in 1969, the center has played a central role in responding to advances in medicine, the biological sciences, and the social sciences by raising ethical questions related to such advances. It conducts research on ethical issues and maintains a library of resources relating to ethics. The center publishes books, papers, guidelines, and the bimonthly journal *Hastings Center Report*.

Institute for Global Ethics

91 Camden Street, Suite 403, Rockland, ME   04841
(207) 594-6658 • fax: (207) 594-6648
e-mail: ethics@globalethics.org
Web site: www.globalethics.org

Dedicated to fostering global ethics, the institute focuses on ethical activities in education, the corporate sector, and public policy. It conducts ethics training seminars, sponsors lectures and workshops, develops curricular materials for elementary and secondary schools, and promotes community-based character education programs. Its resources include articles, reports, and white papers as well as the news publication *Ethics Newsline* and the *Ethicast* podcast.

Josephson Institute of Ethics

9841 Airport Blvd. #300, Los Angeles, CA   90045
(310) 846-4800 • fax: (310) 846-4858
Web site: www.josephsoninstitute.org

The institute's mission is to improve the ethical quality of society by advocating principled reasoning and ethical decision making. It offers training seminars as well as specialized consulting services for businesses. Its Character Counts! coalition promotes character education through the partnership of educational and human-service organizations. The institute publishes materials for teachers, parents, and children and as well as e-newsletters.

Kennedy Institute of Ethics

Healy Hall, 4th Floor, Georgetown University
Washington, DC   20057
(202) 687-8099
Web site: http://kennedyinstitute.georgetown.edu

The institute is a teaching and research center that offers ethical perspectives on major policy issues in the fields of medicine, religion, law, journalism, international affairs, and business. It houses the National Reference Center for Bioethics Literature, produces an online medical ethics database, and conducts regular seminars and courses in bioethics. The institute's publications include the annual *Bibliography of Bioethics*, the quarterly *Kennedy Institute of Ethics Journal*, and the Scope Note Series on specific topics concerning biomedical ethics.

Park Ridge Center for the Study of Health, Faith, and Ethics

205 W. Touhy Ave., Suite 203, Park Ridge, IL   60068-4202
(837) 384-3507 • fax: (837) 384-3557
Web site: www.parkridgecenter.org

The center explores the relationships between health, faith, and ethics, focusing on the religious dimensions of illness and health. It seeks to help clergy, health care professionals, ethicists, educators, and public policy makers address ethical issues and create ethical policies. The center publishes the quarterly *Second Opinion* and the newsletter *e-Ethics*.

Bibliography of Books

Karen Armstrong   *The Case for God.* New York: Knopf, 2009.

Michael Bellomo   *The Stem Cell Divide: The Facts, the Fiction, and the Fear Driving the Greatest Scientific, Political, and Religious Debate of Our Time.* New York: AMACOM, 2006.

Michael Blowfield and Alan Murray   *Corporate Responsibility: A Critical Introduction.* New York: Oxford University Press, 2008.

William H. Colby   *Unplugged: Reclaiming Our Right to Die in America.* New York: AMACON, 2006.

Harvey Cox   *The Future of Faith.* New York: HarperOne, 2009.

Richard Dawkins   *The God Delusion.* New York: Mariner Books, 2008.

Theodore C. Denise, Nicholas P. White, and Sheldon P. Peterfreund   *Great Traditions in Ethics.* Belmont, CA: Thomson/Wadsworth, 2008.

Michael S. Gazzaniga   *The Ethical Brain: The Science of Our Moral Dilemmas.* New York: HarperPerennial, 2006.

Robert P. George and Christopher Tollefsen   *Embryo: A Defense of Human Life.* New York: Doubleday, 2008.

Scott Hahn and Benjamin Wiker
Answering the New Atheism: Dismantling Dawkins' Case Against God. Steubenville, OH: Emmaus Road, 2008.

Eve Harold
Stem Cell Wars: Inside Stories from the Frontlines. New York: Palgrave Macmillan, 2007.

Rob Harrison, Terry Newholm, and Deirdre Shaw
The Ethical Consumer. London: Sage, 2005.

Marc Hauser
Moral Minds: How Nature Designed Our Universal Sense of Right and Wrong. New York: Ecco, 2006.

Roger Highfield and Ian Wilmut
After Dolly: The Promise and Perils of Cloning. New York: Norton, 2006.

Lawrence M. Hinman
Ethics: A Pluralistic Approach to Moral Theory, 4th ed. Belmont, CA: Thomson/Wadsworth, 2008.

Christopher Hitchens
The Portable Atheist: Essential Readings for the Nonbeliever. Philadelphia: Da Capo, 2007.

Richard Holloway
Doubts and Loves: What Is Left of Christianity. Edinburgh: Canongate Books, 2005.

Richard Joyce
The Evolution of Morality. Cambridge, MA: MIT Press, 2006.

Kerry Lynn Macintosh
Illegal Beings: Human Clones and the Law. New York: Cambridge University Press, 2006.

William H. Shaw — *Business Ethics*. Belmont, CA: Thomson/Wadsworth, 2007.

Wesley J. Smith — *Forced Exit: Euthanasia, Assisted Suicide, and the New Duty to Die*. New York: Encounter Books, 2006.

Kathleen Taylor — *Cruelty: Human Evil and the Human Brain*. New York: Oxford University Press, 2009.

David Vogel — *The Market for Virtue: The Potential and Limits of Corporate Social Responsibility*. Washington, DC: Brookings Institution Press, 2005.

Frans de Waal — *The Age of Empathy: Nature's Lessons for a Kinder Society*. New York: Harmony Books, 2009.

Frans de Waal — *Primates and Philosophers: How Morality Evolved*. Princeton, NJ: Princetown University Press, 2006.

Robin Wright — *The Evolution of God*. New York: Little, Brown, 2009.

Index

A

Abortion, 39, 70, 111
Abraham (of the Bible), 37, 83
Abstinence education, 98, 100
Academic dishonesty, 14
Acts (New Testament), 36, 37
Adaptive morality, 87, 91
Age of Reason, 69
Agreeableness, 94
AIDS, 24, 76, 124, 167
Alcohol abuse, 54
Alzheimer's disease, 109, 110, 124
American Academy of Hospice and Palliative Medicine, 138
American Board of Medical Specialties, 130
Amorality, 69–70
Animals, kindness to, 75–76
Antisocial personality disorder, 94
Appel, Jacob M., 149–154
Aristotle, 101–102
Arthritis, 109
Ashley Treatment, 106
Assisted suicide. See Physician-assisted suicide
Association of Northern California Oncologists, 146
Atheism, 79
Australian (newspaper), 16

B

Baby boomers, 109
Beckerman, Wilfred, 22–23
Ben & Jerry's, 170
Benedict XVI (Pope), 81

Biblical ethics/morality, 33–43
application to modernity, 35–36, 38–39
Christian vs. non-Christian belief, 40–43
in the church, 34–35
humanity and, 38–40
New Testament ethics, 38, 39, 40–41
Old Testament morality, 37–38, 148
in the past, 34
physician-assisted suicide and, 144
prophetic stance, 39–40
public stance, 40–43
See also Christians/Christian thought; Jesus Christ; Jews/Judaism
Bill of Rights, 48
Bioethics Center (University of Pennsylvania), 106
Biological roots of ethical behavior, 85–86
Biotechnology, 122–123
Blogs/blogging, 18, 56
Boa, Kenneth, 33–43
The Body Shop, 170
Bono, 167
Branch Davidian religious sect, 48
Brown, Chris, 18–19
Brownback-Landrieu cloning bill, 158, 162
Bullies, 94
Burke, Edmund, 26
See also Contractarianism
Burns, George, 34

Hawaii and, 139
Holland experience, 146–147
hospice care, 129, 131, 138
last-resort options, 131, 136
necessity of, 135–137
New Hampshire and, 139
Oregon lethal medication law, 129, 132, 135–136
palliative care and, 128–130
patient option discussions, 134–135
as secret practice, 133
Supreme Court decision, 137
unacceptability of suffering, 135
VSED practice, 133, 136
Washington (state) and, 139
See also Euthanasia; Passive euthanasia
Physician Orders for Life-Sustaining Treatment (POLST) form, 132
Pinker, Steven, 94, 122–123
Plagiarism, 14
Pluralism, 98
Polar ice caps, melting of, 22
Porter, Gayle, 171
Poverty, 24
Powerful Parent Blog, 56
Praeger, Dennis, 68–77
Praxeology (concept of Mises), 51–52
Pregnancy, 100
Prison Fellowship Ministries, 15
Product (RED) campaign, 167–168, 171
Project Shakti (India), 171–172
Promiscuity, 100
Psalms (Old Testament), 38
Psychopathic personality, 94

Q

Quill, Timothy E., 128–140

R

Raëlian Church, 152–153
Randomness, 47
Rawls, John, 27
Real world orderliness, 45–47
Reason, 32
amorality of, 69–70
belief in goodness vs., 71
complete person vs., 70
data vs., 46
derivations/proposed use of, 44, 49
as divorced from God, 69–71
as hallmark of humanity's potential, 71
mathematics and, 45–46
practical reason subdomain, 50
Reeve, Christopher, 125
Religion, science vs. (argument), 46
Report Card on the Ethics of American Youth (2008), 14, 15–16
Rihanna, 18–19
"Rights" of humanity, 48
Rogatz, Peter, 137
Romans (New Testament), 37, 40
Rosenman, Mark, 167

S

Savitz, Andy, 171, 172
Schafer, Arthur, 107
Schiavo, Terry, 142
Schultz, Norman R., 28